ERIC ROSSWOOD

QUEER CHEER

ACTIVITIES, ADVICE, AND AFFIRMATIONS FOR LGBTQ+ TEENS

Published by Mango Publishing, a division of Mango Publishing Group, Inc.

Layout & Design: Jodie Anders, www.QueerCheerBook.com
Pomodoro® Technique, © Copyright 2021 Social and Political Psychology Lab

Queer Cheer: Activities, Advice, and Affirmations for LGBTQ+ Teens

Library of Congress Cataloging-in-Publication number: 2023952620
ISBN: (pb) 978-1-68481-480-0 (e) 978-1-68481-481-7
BISAC category code YAN032000, YOUNG ADULT NONFICTION / LGBTQ+

Queer Cheer is a thought-provoking book intended to give you a burst of positivity and confidence. Some content includes discussions of abandonment, anxiety, body image, bullying, depression, eating disorders, family rejection, gender discrimination, homophobia, mental health, religious trauma, transphobia, and suicide. We encourage readers who may be sensitive to these elements to note this and take care of themselves.

The information provided in this book is based on the research, insights, and experiences of the authors. Every effort has been made to provide accurate and up-to-date information; however, neither the authors nor the publisher warrants the information provided is free of factual error. This book is not intended to diagnose, treat, or cure any medical condition or disease, nor is it intended as a substitute for professional medical care. All matters regarding your health should be supervised by a qualified healthcare professional. The author and publisher disclaim all liability for any adverse effects arising out of or relating to the use or application of the information or advice provided in this book.

TABLE OF CONTENTS

• Welcome • The Authors • Teen Voices • Using Affirmations

IDENTITY P. 9
• Who Am I? • My Queer Identities
• Coming Out • Spirituality

HELPFUL HABITS P. 38
• Prioritizing You • Self-Care
• Nurturing Your Body • Managing Emotions
• Changing Perspectives

CONFIDENCE P. 73
• Believing in Yourself • Body Image
• Getting in the Zone • Stepping Out

RELATIONSHIPS P. 100
• Healthy Relationships • Being Accepted for You
• What Makes a Family? • Quality Friendships
• Love, Romance & Intimacy

SCHOOL P. 134
• Educational Environment
• Promoting Inclusion
• Filling in Education Gaps

OUR COMMUNITY P. 156
• Navigating Spaces • Our Fabulous Culture
• Finding Your Space • Supporting Our Community
• Activism

SUCCESS & FUTURE P. 190
• Dream It, Be It • Achieving Goals
• Growth Mindset

• Afterword • Resources

Dear Reader,

We're so glad you're queer...we mean here. Well, actually, we're glad you're queer and here, because that's the whole point of this book—celebrating and uplifting queer teens! Through our conversations with queer teens across the country, we have come to realize that, although they face unique challenges in life, their experiences have given rise to unique and powerful voices. You, too, are unique and powerful! You have something special to offer because no one has your perspective, experience, and personality, and with that you can change the world.

Consider this book your queer teen survival kit to aid you on your journey, whether you're looking for a bit of inspiration, aid in facing struggles, or extra joy in queer and teen life. This book isn't your typical advice book; it's a positivity book! Because, let's face it, we could all use a little Queer Cheer now and then. After a short introduction, you'll encounter pages with activities, tips, questions, and affirmations to inspire you toward positive change. Pick a section you need, or read it from cover to cover; it's up to you. The important thing is to find what works best for you, because you deserve to feel your best! So, are you ready for your inner glow-up? Then let's get started!

Your Queer Cheer Duo,
Eric & Jodie

MEET THE AUTHORS!

HELLO MY NAME IS
JODIE
(SHE/HER) BI/DEMI

HELLO MY NAME IS
ERIC
(HE/HIM) GAY

Hi! I'm Eric, and I'm totally, unequivocally, 100 percent gay! My husband and I have two amazing kids, and we love to go on family adventures where we can explore new things and take in the wonders of the world.

My Favorite Affirmation: "Today is going to be a good day because I'm going to make it a good day."

It reminds me that I have the power to control my own destiny. I can make good things happen for me, and even if something bad happens, I can choose how I react to it.

Hi there, I'm Jodie! I'm bisexual and demisexual. I live in Los Angeles with my two adorable cats. I love comic conventions, concerts, musical theater, singing with friends, and traveling the world.

My Favorite Affirmation: "I strive for progress, not perfection. No one is perfect."

I have struggled with making things "perfect" in the hope that others will accept my efforts and, therefore, accept me. This affirmation reminds me to let go of that subjective illusion and, instead, focus on the joy and growth of my unique contributions.

Hi

ALIA, 17 (THEY/THEM), GENDERQUEER, QUEER — MASSACHUSETTS

ADRIAN, 19 (SHE/HER), BI — ILLINOIS

ADARA, 18 (THEY/THEM), AGENDER, PANROMANTIC, ACE — COLORADO

CHACE, 17 (HE/HIM), QUEER — RHODE ISLAND

LIS, 17 (ANY), QUEER — ARIZONA

EVAN, 18 (HE/THEY), GAY — ILLINOIS

CADENCE, 13 (ANY), GENDERFLUID, PAN — CALIFORNIA

ELIXIR, 16 (THEY/THEM), OMNI, GENDERFLUID — IOWA

CALLAHAN, 18 (HE/HIM), TRANS — ARIZONA

QUEER TEEN VOICES THROUGHOUT THIS BOOK

NACEY, 19 (SHE/HER), BI/QUEER — ILLINOIS

LUCY, 19 (SHE/HER), LESBIAN — HAWAII

JACKIE, 13 (HE/HIM), BI — CALIFORNIA

JACKSON, 18 (HE/HIM), TRANS, NONBINARY, POLY, PAN, ARO, DEMI — RHODE ISLAND

ZIE, 17 (ANY), PAN, GENDERFLUID — ARIZONA

KATIE, 14 (THEY/THEM), PAN, POLY — ARIZONA

CONSTANCE, 19, (SHE/HER), TRANS — CALIFORNIA

LUKE, 16 (HE/HIM), BI — NEW YORK

PERCY, 18 (THEY/THEM), GENDERFLUID, QUEER — MASSACHUSETTS

SHALOM, 18 (HE/HIM), BI — WASHINGTON D.C.

PARKER, 16 (HE/HIM), TRANS, ACE, PAN — INDIANA

How to Use Affirmations

Affirmations are positive statements we say to motivate ourselves, encourage positive changes in our lives, and/or boost our self-esteem. When practiced daily, affirmations can help us shift our mindset and make it easier to resist negative thoughts, overcome anxiety, and increase self-love.

Have you ever been told that your identity wasn't real, or maybe you've heard someone say something negative about queer people in general? Of course, none of this is true, but words matter, and continuously hearing negative things like this could potentially cause a person to have self-doubt. We may even find ourselves confirming those lies with negative self-talk. That's why affirmations are so important, and it's why we need to say them out loud. It's critical that we hear positive, affirming things about ourselves to prevent the negative thoughts from taking over.

But let us be perfectly queer. Affirmations are not mystical spells you say to yourself once in the mirror while waiting for a fairy godmother to—POOF!—magically appear and change your whole belief system. It takes TIME to actually get your brain on board with the words you're repeating, and it takes EFFORT, too. But don't worry. We're here to help. At the end of each section, we have something we like to call Rainbow Affirmations. This is where we include affirmations you can use to get started on your journey to increasing your queer positivity! So, are you ready to get started and increase your personal pride? Okay then. Let's go!

TIPS FOR GETTING THE MOST OUT OF YOUR AFFIRMATIONS

1. Think about negative thoughts you want to vaporize from your brain or areas where you could use a boost of mental positivity. Prioritize a few to work on.

2. Pick affirmations that counter those negative thoughts, or ones that lift you up in those areas. Try picking ones that resonate with you. If you're not feeling the affirmations listed, try creating your own by writing down a counterargument to your negative thought.

3. Once you've picked your affirmations, write them down and put them someplace where you can refer to them daily, such as on your bathroom mirror, on your laptop, in your textbooks, or inside your locker.

4. Say your affirmation out loud, several times. If you can, look directly into a mirror and tell yourself! It's okay if you're not quite believing the words or you feel uncomfortable at first. Stick with it. You'll get there!

5. Repeat these affirmations daily and try to be patient. You'll find they slowly change your pattern of thinking!

Knowing who you are helps you find your place in the world, where you can build confidence and make the best decisions for YOU! Take time to look inside and discover yourself, from your roots to your queer identity, to your hopes and dreams. When you do this, you'll uncover a multifaceted gem born to shine!

HOW DO THESE IDENTITY TYPES PLAY A PART IN WHO YOU ARE?

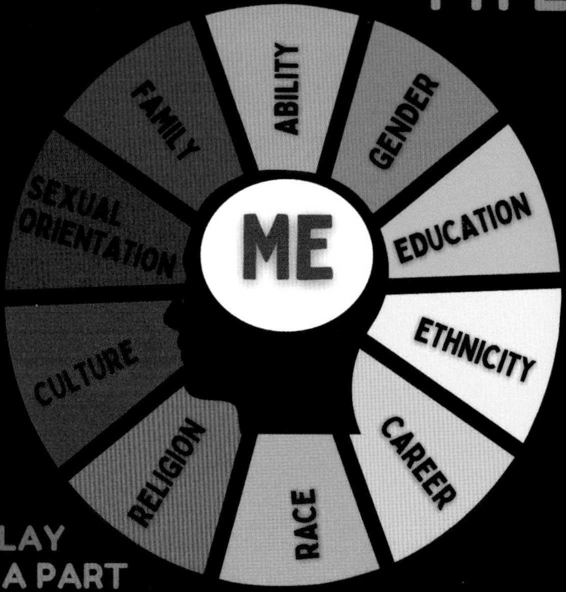

ME

- ABILITY
- GENDER
- EDUCATION
- ETHNICITY
- CAREER
- RACE
- RELIGION
- CULTURE
- SEXUAL ORIENTATION
- FAMILY

WHO AM I?

You might be wondering who the heck you are, and that's totally valid. It's an intriguing question you'll be exploring your whole life. **Your identity is made up of lots of different aspects**, such as race, ability, sexual orientation, and gender identity. Some of these things you can't change, but others might shift over time. As these aspects intersect and evolve, they result in a beautiful, ever-changing rainbow of possibilities! The key is to take the time to explore and adore every part of your legendary self. When you do that, you'll see how awesome and unique you really are. **There really is no one in this world quite like you**, so don't be afraid to let your true colors shine!

"WE'RE ALL DIFFERENT IN MANY WAYS AND ALIKE IN MANY WAYS AND SPECIAL IN SOME SORT OF WAY."
—LARRY KRAMER

Conversations On IDENTITY

CONSTANCE (19)

"I'm mixed race, so me being trans does intersect with that to some degree, and being a trans woman of color is a huge part of my identity because trans WOC were among the first to stand up and fight for queer rights!"

PERCY (18)

"I have ADHD and being neurodivergent is a big part of my identity in addition to my queerness. I am a very creatively minded person in part due to the unique way in which having ADHD affects my life. It is a big part of how I make connections with others and seek to find my way in the world."

JACKSON (18)

"Almost all of my friends are queer, so I don't think about my identity much in my day-to-day. But I realize that being queer is a notable difference between me and a lot of the other people in the world, and it makes up a lot of who I am."

CALLAHAN (18)

"Singing has always been a huge part of my life, and I also play a little piano. Music in general is a big part of my identity."

SHALOM (18)

"I kind of grew up thinking that before I'm queer, I'm black, in the sense that if I enter any space where it's full of white cishet people, I can just pretend to not be gay, but I can't pretend to not be black. But the reality is that I'm always going to be black and queer, even if I'm pretending to not be queer."

LUCY (19)

"I think knowing myself really well, and knowing what I enjoy doing, helps me navigate life."

True or False?

People should be defined by their..

	True	False
Integrity	☑	☐
Values/Morals	☑	☐
Style	☑	☐
Abilities	☐	☑
Housing	☐	☑
Failures/Mistakes	☐	☑
Beliefs	☑	☐
Appearance	☐	☑
Number of Friends	☐	☑
Genetics	☐	☑
Relationship Status	☐	☑

1 PERSONALITY QUIZZES

Personality quizzes range from fun quizzes that assign you a TV character to in-depth quizzes that help you identify personality characteristics, assets, and communication styles. Search the web for a quiz that intrigues you and take it! When you're done, see if there's something you learned about yourself.

Try These ACTIVITIES

2 SOCIAL MEDIA EXAMINATION

Scroll through your social media profile. Does your bio accurately reflect who you are? Do your posts or photos best reflect your true personality and style? Why or why not?

3 DESCRIBE ME

Ask a few people who know you well to each list three to five words that describe you. Evaluate the lists. Do you agree with them? Do all the lists describe you in the same way? If not, could the differences be influenced by an identity shift, relationship difference, or other dynamic?

SELF QUEERY

QUEER QUESTIONS

WHAT ASPECTS OF YOUR IDENTITY DO YOU FEEL MOST CONNECTED TO? DOES THIS CHANGE IN DIFFERENT ENVIRONMENTS?

ASK YOURSELF

QUEER QUESTIONS

HOW WOULD YOU DESCRIBE YOURSELF TO SOMEONE WHO HAS NEVER MET YOU? WHAT IS IMPORTANT TO INCLUDE OR NOT INCLUDE?

ASK YOURSELF

QUEER QUESTIONS

WHAT ARE YOUR MOST IMPORTANT VALUES AND MORALS?

ASK YOURSELF

QUEER QUESTIONS

WHEN YOU MEET SOMEONE FOR THE FIRST TIME, WHAT IMPRESSIONS DO YOU GIVE THEM? DO THOSE IMPRESSIONS CHANGE AS THEY GET TO KNOW YOU?

ASK YOURSELF

CARE TO SHARE?

#ShareQueerCheer

RAINBOW AFFIRMATIONS

I embrace and celebrate all aspects of my identity.

I am not afraid to express myself and my unique personality.

I am authentic and true to myself.

There is no one else like me, and that makes me unique and awesome.

I am who I am, and that is a gift.

I have all the time I need to explore who I am.

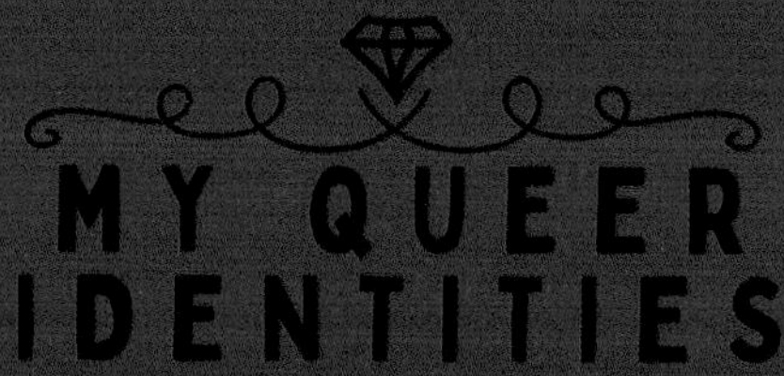

MY QUEER IDENTITIES

Defining your queer identity can sometimes be confusing, but you have your whole life to figure it out. **There is no requirement to find perfectly fitting labels or to use them at all.** You may be familiar with a few labels (like gay, nonbinary, etc.), but feel free to browse through additional ones to see if any resonate with you. If you haven't figured it all out yet, that's okay—you don't have to explain yourself to anyone. **Take your time, explore what works best for you, and express your orientation and gender however you choose!**

<u>SEX:</u> A CATEGORIZATION BASED ON THE PHYSICAL DIFFERENCES OF MALES, FEMALES, AND INTERSEX PEOPLE.

<u>GENDER:</u> A SOCIAL CONSTRUCT USED TO CLASSIFY CHARACTERISTICS, EXPRESSIONS, AND ROLES.

<u>SEXUAL ORIENTATION:</u> THE ROMANTIC, EMOTIONAL, AND/OR SEXUAL ATTRACTION (OR LACK THEREOF) TO OTHERS.

<u>GENDER IDENTITY:</u> A PERSONAL SENSE OF ONE'S OWN GENDER, WHICH MAY OR MAY NOT CORRELATE WITH THEIR PHYSICAL APPEARANCE, GENDER EXPRESSION, OR SEX.

REMEMBER...

GENDER EXPRESSION <u>NEVER</u> INVALIDATES YOUR GENDER IDENTITY.

YOUR PARTNER'S GENDER DOES NOT DETERMINE YOUR SEXUAL ORIENTATION.

EXPERIENCES YOU'VE HAD (OR HAVEN'T HAD) DO NOT INVALIDATE YOUR IDENTITY.

Conversations On QUEER IDENTITIES

PARKER (16)

"I was never interested in makeup and a lot of things that people would classify as girl things. I was always interested in doing whatever my dad was doing, and in male characters from books or TV shows. Then things kind of just started clicking, and then the name clicked."

ADARA (18)

"When I started interacting on the internet, I didn't want to use my gender at the time, so I just used they/them pronouns and hid the fact that I was a woman for safety, and I liked that so much more than she/her. I realized what I felt about my body was actually dysphoria and I was like, 'OMG! The pieces are coming together!' "

CALLAHAN (18)

"In middle school, I started watching trans men online and seeing how they felt. It was very similar to how I felt—and I was like, 'Maybe I'm trans,' but then I would convince myself, 'No, you're just a lesbian. You're not trans. That's not real'—And then, about two years ago, I was talking to my friends, and they were like, 'Let me use he/him in a sentence' —and it clicked."

PERCY (18)

"Took about two years to end up where I am now. I settled on queer because that encapsulates things for me. I'm confident where I am now, but I know things can change and that's okay. I don't feel restricted by labels."

JACKSON (18)

"Even though my labels have changed over the years, I have pretty much felt the same way the whole time. To me, the labels don't really decide who I am or how I feel about that. I just like having the words that I can use to explain to other people."

ALIA (17)

"I went online and did those stupid 'Am I Gay?' quizzes that don't work, but they're super funny. They always ask questions like 'Would you date someone the same gender as you?' and it's like...if I knew my answer to that, why would I be here? It goes to show that no one except yourself can say who you are."

ZIE (17)

"I go by gender fluid because I don't know my gender. It's not important to me. I've never found gender important in any way, shape, or form. So, I go by whatever anyone calls me, and I call it good."

SHALOM (18)

"I figured out I was bisexual when I was eight years old. I had a crush on Prince Eric from the LITTLE MERMAID cartoon, and also on Andrew Garfield and Emma Stone in SPIDER-MAN. That's how I kind of figured it out. I didn't learn the terminology until I was in middle school."

Conversations On NAME CHANGES

You have the power to create the names, titles, and words you need to be affirmed and respected. Some people choose a new name when they feel like their birthname doesn't match their gender identity. If you choose to change your name, it's up to you how and when you want to do this. You also get to choose in which spaces you use your new name, and whether or not to change it legally if you can. You can also decide on your courtesy titles, such as Mr., Ms., Mx., Mre., etc. Here are a few stories from teens who have changed their names.

HELLO MY NAME IS *Callahan*

"I wanted to keep the same nickname as my legal name 'cause I didn't come out to my family first. I was going through baby name websites, and I found Callahan. My friend was also looking for names for me and texted me Callahan at the same time I saw it, and I was like alright, that's it. That's my big strong man name."

HELLO MY NAME IS *Percy*

"People often assume I chose my name as a reference to Percy Jackson, but in reality, it's in honor of my favorite Greek Goddess, Persephone. She is both the Goddess of Spring and the Queen of the Underworld. She doesn't let labels, or the expectations of others, define her identity."

HELLO MY NAME IS *Constance*

"I picked my name because of a character from a book that I like. At the time, I related very much to this character because she was a confident young woman with a killer sense of style and humor. I wanted to be like her, so changing my name to hers felt like the beginning of manifesting this new self into the world."

DEADNAMING: WHEN AN INDIVIDUAL REFERS TO THE BIRTH NAME, GIVEN NAME, OR OLD NAME SOMEONE USED PRIOR TO GENDER TRANSITION.

LABELS & TERMS

The LGBTQ+ community is incredibly diverse, encompassing a wide range of subcultures, identities, orientations, and genders. This is not an exhaustive list. Language is a powerful tool, and terms evolve all the time. We encourage you to look up more labels and terms online to see if any resonate with you.

LESBIAN: A woman who is attracted to women. Some nonbinary people also use this term.

GAY: A man who is attracted to men. Also used as an umbrella term similar to queer.

BISEXUAL: Someone attracted to more than one gender.

TRANSGENDER: A person whose gender identity doesn't align with their sex assigned at birth.

QUEER: An umbrella term used to express a spectrum of identities and orientations that are not considered mainstream.

INTERSEX: Term used to describe people born with chromosomes or reproductive or sexual anatomy not considered typically male or female.

ASEXUAL: Experiencing little/no sexual attraction. Sub-umbrellas exist, such as demi-sexual/grey-sexual, where attraction relies on emotional bonds.

AROMANTIC: Experiencing little/no romantic attraction. Sub-umbrellas exist to define the spectrum of attraction, such as grey-romantic and demi-romantic.

CISGENDER: A person whose gender identity matches their sex assigned at birth.

PANSEXUAL: Attraction regardless of gender identity.

POLYAMOROUS: Engaging in multiple relationships with consent of all involved.

OMNI-SEXUAL: Attracted to all genders. Gender may still play a role in attraction.

NONBINARY: A person whose gender identity and/or expression does not conform to the gender binary of man or woman. A nonbinary person may identify as both, somewhere in between, or outside of the binary. Some examples include agender, bigender, and genderqueer.

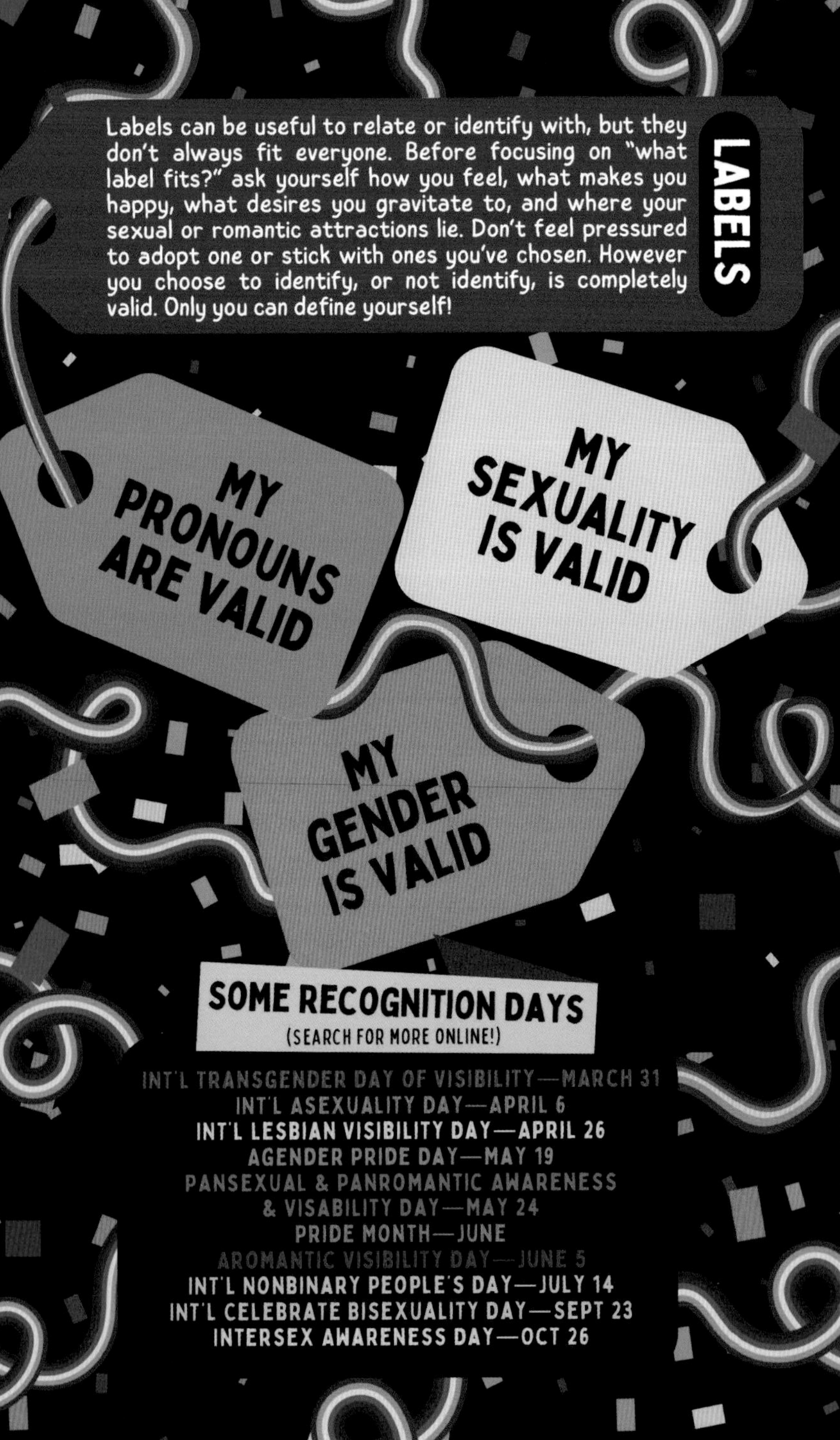
LABELS
Labels can be useful to relate or identify with, but they don't always fit everyone. Before focusing on "what label fits?" ask yourself how you feel, what makes you happy, what desires you gravitate to, and where your sexual or romantic attractions lie. Don't feel pressured to adopt one or stick with ones you've chosen. However you choose to identify, or not identify, is completely valid. Only you can define yourself!
MY PRONOUNS ARE VALID
MY SEXUALITY IS VALID
MY GENDER IS VALID
SOME RECOGNITION DAYS
(SEARCH FOR MORE ONLINE!)
INT'L TRANSGENDER DAY OF VISIBILITY—MARCH 31
INT'L ASEXUALITY DAY—APRIL 6
INT'L LESBIAN VISIBILITY DAY—APRIL 26
AGENDER PRIDE DAY—MAY 19
PANSEXUAL & PANROMANTIC AWARENESS & VISABILITY DAY—MAY 24
PRIDE MONTH—JUNE
AROMANTIC VISIBILITY DAY—JUNE 5
INT'L NONBINARY PEOPLE'S DAY—JULY 14
INT'L CELEBRATE BISEXUALITY DAY—SEPT 23
INTERSEX AWARENESS DAY—OCT 26

Try These **ACTIVITIES**

1 MAKE YOUR CHARACTER PROFILE

Some writers find it helpful to create profile sheets when envisioning new characters for their stories. Find a profile sheet online and fill it out with your personal details. What is your style, what are your interests, goals, etc.? Then, fill out another profile sheet for the partner you'd like to have. When you're done, evaluate. What do the profiles tell you about yourself?

2 LET'S HEAR IT

Talk to a close friend or someone you trust, and have them refer to you with different pronouns during the conversation. Pay close attention to how it makes you feel.

3 CAN YOU RELATE

Read a book or watch a movie where the main character is queer. Evaluate whether or not you identify with their feelings.

SELF QUEERY
QUEER QUESTIONS
WHEN YOU IMAGINE A PARTNER, WHAT PHYSICAL AND NONPHYSICAL CHARACTERISTICS APPEAL TO YOU?
ASK YOURSELF
QUEER QUESTIONS
DO YOU FEEL LIKE YOU NEED TO FIND A LABEL THAT DEFINES YOU? WHY OR WHY NOT?
ASK YOURSELF
QUEER QUESTIONS
WHAT GENDER ROLES AND STEREOTYPES RESONATE WITH YOU? WHICH ONES DON'T?
ASK YOURSELF
QUEER QUESTIONS
WHAT LABELS OR DEFINITIONS FEEL MOST ACCURATE WHEN CONSIDERING YOUR GENDER AND ROMANTIC/PHYSICAL ATTRACTIONS? WHY?
ASK YOURSELF
CARE TO SHARE?
#ShareQueerCheer

RAINBOW AFFIRMATIONS

I can name, explore, and discover my identities when and how I want.

My orientation and identity are part of what makes me magnificent.

I can choose which labels to use, or not use, to identify myself.

My pronouns are valid and deserve to be respected.

I do not have to prove or justify my sexual orientation or gender identity to anyone.

I'm allowed to change. This doesn't mean everything I said or felt before was wrong or untrue.

COMING OUT

Revealing your true self begins with accepting and celebrating all of your marvelous identities. Even if you're not quite ready to come out yet, **always remember that being queer is completely normal and valid—heck, it's downright fabulous!** It's understandable to feel nervous about coming out, especially when you don't know how others may react, but remember, you don't have to share with folks you don't trust. Evaluate each situation for safety and comfort and feel free to share only when you're ready.

This is **your** personal journey and how you share your truth is up to you. Some people make a grand announcement to everyone they know, while others share their truth through a series of small conversations, expressions, or even appearance changes. Either way, you'll likely come out multiple times as you meet new people throughout your life. **If you're considering coming out, it may help to know that many in our community have reported benefits, such as boosts to self-esteem and confidence.** However you choose to come out, don't forget to celebrate every time you share your truth. Your bravery to stand up and be you is legendary!

REMEMBER...

It is never okay to out someone without their permission

"I WANTED TO BE OUT SO I COULD RELAX AND BE ME."
—MELISSA ETHERIDGE

Conversations On COMING OUT

NACEY (19)

"In the middle of freshman year, I was like, 'I think I'm attracted to women.' A girl I was friends with in high school was telling people I had a crush on her, and she was weirded out by it, and that hurt. She was making up stories of me coming on to her. A queer person's biggest fear is having her friend think they're attracted to her."

CADENCE (13)

"Coming out to my family was hard because I didn't know how they would react. Some people in my family are toxic, and I didn't want them to know. It got around and they found out. It's hard to have family members not accept you and call you names because of it. You just have to realize, if they won't accept you for who you are, that's their problem, not yours."

ADARA (18)

"I was at a family party once, and we were being separated by genders for family photos. I wasn't comfortable when they wanted me on the girl's side. My mom asked if I wanted to be with the boys, and I was like, 'No, it's not that either.' A woman asked if I was nonbinary, and she got me a they/them/theirs pronoun pin. So, instead of officially coming out—I put the pin on. My dad asked me about it, and he was like, 'Do you want me to tell Mom about it?' and I was like, 'Yes, please.'"

JACKSON (18)

"I have awesome friends. When I came out to them as trans, I just sort of told them and they were like, 'Oh, okay. That's cool. We'll change pronouns.' I've made new friends at school since then. They kind of joined our group and me being trans was already known and accepted in our circle, so I haven't really had to specifically come out to friends in a long time. It's always been pretty casual."

ALIA (17)

"I'm very lucky in my experience that I have supportive parents, so coming out wasn't a very difficult process and I never had a ton of inner turmoil. Also, seeing people around me who were more comfortable with themselves really helped, too."

LUCY (19)

"I just don't come out to difficult people like my aunt. It's just not her business. She doesn't need to know and it's easier that way. But for like my dad, I hung up a Pride flag in my room and was like, 'Can you come kill a bug for me?' And then I was like, 'Also, I like girls,' and he was like, 'Okay.' That's pretty much it."

Conversations On COMING OUT

CHACE (17)

"I never really felt a need to come out to be seen. I live with my mom, and no matter who I decide to be in a relationship with, my mom is going to support that. And so, I don't really feel the need to kind of explicitly say, 'Oh, I'm this,' or 'I'm that,' because I know whatever I do, she's gonna be cool with it."

CALLAHAN (18)

"When I came out, my family told me I couldn't be trans and that I was just being influenced by the media. My friends told me it was a phase. It was so frustrating because this was something I was so sure about, but other people couldn't see it, and I couldn't make them see it. Most of my friends and family came around, though. Overall, things have definitely improved from when I first came out. My mental health is better than it's ever been, and I'm accepted in most aspects of my life now."

EVAN (18)

"A lot of my friends were out and confident with who they were, so I decided to come out to them first. Even though they were queer, it was still scary because I had never told anyone before. To gain courage, I watched coming out videos on YouTube and it helped a lot."

CONSTANCE (19)

"I came out to my family last, because I cared very much about what they thought. I wanted to make sure I was 100 percent sure before I told them. They accepted me and agreed to use my name and pronouns, though at first my mom was grieving the loss of her son. But I think that's completely normal and that it's important to have empathy for the older people who you choose to share your true self with. Unless they dismiss you, obviously."

LIS (17)

"Coming out to my parents was a little weird because I identified as pan when I came out, and they didn't understand what that meant because they thought it meant I was gay. I was dating a man at the time, which was even more confusing for them. I explained what being pan meant and both of my parents were very supportive of that."

PERCY (18)

"I came out to my grandpa because I wanted him to come to my graduation, but I was going to graduate as Percy, and he didn't know me by that name. He was a lot more chill with my name, but it was harder for him to use my pronouns. I don't mind if people make mistakes with my pronouns, though, as long as they actively try."

"YOU DON'T HAVE TO COME OUT TO EVERYBODY! Oftentimes, I see a lot of younger trans kids getting down on themselves because their homophobic uncle won't use their name or pronouns—or maybe it's a friend or teacher. There are times when your peace is worth protecting more so than revealing your true self to everybody. What's helped me is to stop thinking of it as "coming out" and more like "welcoming in." Share your true self with the people who deserve to know it—to the people whose support actually matters to you. At the end of the day, if coming out to your parent or classmate will stymie your comfort and your peace, it isn't worth it. I live authentically as myself every single day, and there are some people who still refer to me as a boy because I choose not to share my true self with them. Not because I'm insecure or worried or any less trans, but because it would only complicate things. When you think of it as welcoming people in as opposed to coming out, YOU have the power and control."

- Constance

TIPS FOR COMING OUT

- Plan ahead and determine safety.
- Test the waters by gauging their response to:
  - A current LGBTQ+ topic or celebrity.
  - Asking what to say to a queer friend.
- Decide the easiest way to share: text, email, in person, phone?
- Plan a time and a safe place that puts you at ease.
- Practice the conversation and anticipate questions.
- Have someone ready to call/text for support or celebration.

Prefer a more creative way to come out? How about something fun and unique like this?

Write a song and sing it
Wear a shirt or pin with your pronouns
Have people guess during charades
Put rainbow flag/heart emojis in your social media profile
Carve it into a Halloween pumpkin
Plan a scavenger hunt to an announcement banner
Spell it out in a word game
Write it on your coffee cup

OCTOBER 11 IS NATIONAL COMING OUT DAY!

The term "coming out" was first used in the late nineteenth century and is borrowed from the debutante balls where elite young women came out into high society.

1 GET INSPIRED

Watch online videos where other people discuss their coming out stories.

2 ROLE PLAY

If you are planning to come out to someone, and you are nervous about doing so, try role playing with a trusted friend or family member first.

3 JOURNAL IT

Sometimes it's easier to get our thoughts out when we write them down. Try coming out in a journal or diary first.

Dear Diary, there's something I've been wanting to tell you...

STRONGER TOGETHER

SELF QUEERY
QUEER QUESTIONS
IN WHAT SPACES OF YOUR LIFE (SCHOOL, HOME, WORK, ETC.) DO YOU HIDE YOUR QUEER IDENTITIES AND WHY?
ASK YOURSELF
QUEER QUESTIONS
WHAT DO YOU IMAGINE IT WOULD FEEL LIKE TO BE OUT?
ASK YOURSELF
QUEER QUESTIONS
WHAT WOULD MAKE IT EASIER FOR YOU TO COME OUT?
ASK YOURSELF
QUEER QUESTIONS
IS THERE SOMEONE YOU WANT TO COME OUT TO BUT HAVEN'T YET? IF SO, WHAT IS YOUR HESITATION? CAN YOU DO SOMETHING TO MAKE IT EASIER TO COME OUT TO THEM?
ASK YOURSELF
CARE TO SHARE?
#ShareQueerCheer

RAINBOW AFFIRMATIONS

My pronouns are valid, and they are not "too complicated."

By being visible and living my truth, I inspire those around me to do the same.

Today, I have the courage to be myself and tell my truth.

I am valid and wonderful no matter who knows or accepts my truth.

I have the power to share, or not share, information about my identity with whom I choose.

I embrace the parts of myself that I have kept hidden from others.

SPIRITUALITY

There are many different belief systems, ranging from those who worship one or more gods to individuals who don't follow any deities. There are also agnostics, people who follow nature-based religions, and those who have no beliefs at all. All of these are completely valid because **spiritual belief is a personal experience unique to each individual.**

Religious communities and the queer community don't always see eye to eye, and some institutions and their followers have been downright awful to people in the LGBTQ+ community, but it's important to remember that these people do not speak for all faiths or spiritual places, and **no one has the right to judge or impose their beliefs on anyone else.** If you have religious trauma and you choose to stay away from religion altogether, that's totally understandable. If you are currently trying to explore your beliefs in a way that reconciles them with your queer identities, that's completely valid, too. Your spiritual journey is between you and your higher power (if you believe in one), and you are allowed to define your beliefs without judgment. It may even help anchor you in rough waters.

If you're looking for a place to explore your spirituality in an affirming way, just know there are welcoming spiritual spaces and faiths that serve our queer community. There are even virtual services available! It's okay to explore a faith that is different from your family or friends or even decide faith is not for you altogether. In the end, the spiritual path you take is YOUR personal choice.

"SO LET ME BE CLEAR: I'M PROUD TO BE GAY, AND I CONSIDER BEING GAY AMONG THE GREATEST GIFTS GOD HAS GIVEN ME." —TIM COOK

Conversations On SPIRITUALITY

EVAN (18)

"I grew up in a Presbyterian church and they are very accepting. My pastor is bisexual, and once a month she wears a rainbow stole. It's great because it lets queer people know they are welcome. On the first Sunday of Pride month, they do a sermon about Pride and talk about how it's okay to be who you are. They say things like, 'God wants you to express yourself,' and 'God wouldn't create you just to hate you.' If you're looking for an accepting church, they do exist. You just have to look to find them."

NACEY (19)

"There was a lot of talk when I was growing up about queer communities and how it wasn't God's plan and it's wrong. My mom tried to keep me away from all the stuff Jehovah's Witnesses believe, and she did a good job of letting me understand religion without it being pushed on me. There were years where I was like, 'God's not going to love me and that's fine.' Then, around seventeen, I didn't believe in God. Now I'm back to where I don't know what I believe in, and I'm still discovering that."

CONSTANCE (19)

"When you grow up being told that God will love you unconditionally, under certain conditions, it really warps the way you think about yourself. I grew up so confused about why I was like this—why I was a boy who felt like a woman inside. I prayed night after night for God to take this sin away, as my pastors suggested, but no luck. Eventually, I thought, 'Every single time I ask God for help, I end up having to help myself anyway, so what's even the point?' which led me to renouncing my faith. Now I believe that only I have the power to save myself."

PARKER (16)

"A member of my church youth group basically told me that I was a mistake from God because of who I am. After that, it took a while to interact with the church. Eventually, I was able to, but I was in therapy. I had to put a lot of trust in my faith, my church, and the people around me. It was easier said than done. But I try to find people who have dealt with something similar and support me and my faith. I felt a lot better after I really figured out who I was. After that, a lot of things fell into place."

ADRIAN (19)

"I am not religious, but I do find myself in touch with some type of spirituality. I grew up in the Unitarian Universalist church and I learned much in that church about what it means to be part of society and to help nurture my community."

LGBTQ+ SPIRITUAL LEADERS

Some queer people have become leaders in their faith. Here are a few!

Bishop Gene Robinson—First openly gay person to be a consecrated bishop in the Episcopal Church.
Rabbi Abby Stein—Jewish trans activist and educator who founded a support group for trans people from Orthodox Jewish backgrounds.
Sister Mahdia Lynn—A disabled transgender Shi'a Muslim and cofounder of Masjid al-Rabia, an LGBTQ+ affirming, anti-racist, accessible, and woman-centered mosque.
Ben Schilaty—A BYU instructor and honor code administrator who wrote a book about being a gay Latter-day Saint and discusses his experience in a podcast.
Father Robert Carter—Cofounder of the National LGBTQ Task Force and one of the first Roman Catholic priests to publicly come out as gay.
Rabbi Rachel Timoner—Lesbian senior rabbi of a Reform congregation who supports youth leadership, immigration, and justice reform.
Reverend angel Kyodo williams—A queer, mixed-race American Buddhist and sensei who founded Transformative Change to prevent activist burnout through spiritual grounding.
Daayiee Abdullah—First openly gay imam in the US. A Muslim activist who performed same-sex weddings and led prayers for AIDS victims when few would.
Archbishop Carl Bean—Founder of Unity Fellowship of Christ Church for openly gay and lesbian African Americans.

If you're looking for a queer-friendly spiritual place, contact your local LGBTQ+ center for recommendations, or explore resources online! The HRC has a great list here: hrc.org/resources/faith-resources

Try These ACTIVITIES

1 CELEBRATION TIME

Pick a holiday from your own religion or another religion to study for a queer connection and then celebrate it in your own unique way. What is the core value of the holiday? How can you tie it to the values of the queer community?

2 LISTEN UP

Search for affirming queer religious or spiritual podcasts and listen to them to see if there's something that inspires you. If you want to take it a step further, listen to ones from different faiths/beliefs. Analyze their similarities and differences.

3 TALK TO LEADERS

Interview a religious leader from a queer-affirming place of worship and ask what passages, texts, or scriptures can be used to support the queer community. If you have trouble finding a queer-affirming place near you, consider emailing one to set up a phone or virtual interview.

STRONGER TOGETHER

SELF QUEERY
QUEER QUESTIONS
WHAT ROLE DOES FAITH PLAY IN SETTING YOUR OWN PERSONAL VALUES, BELIEFS, AND MORALS?
ASK YOURSELF
QUEER QUESTIONS
DOES FAITH PLAY A ROLE IN YOUR EXPLORATION OF SEXUALITY OR GENDER IDENTITY? WHY OR WHY NOT?
ASK YOURSELF
QUEER QUESTIONS
IF YOU SUFFER FROM RELIGIOUS TRAUMA, WHAT IS SOMETHING THAT MIGHT HELP YOU HEAL?
ASK YOURSELF
QUEER QUESTIONS
IN WHAT WAYS CAN YOU USE FAITH AND ITS TEXTS TO AFFIRM PEOPLE IN THE LGBTQ+ COMMUNITY?
ASK YOURSELF
CARE TO SHARE?
#ShareQueerCheer

RAINBOW AFFIRMATIONS

My creator loves me just the way I am, queer and all!

Other people don't dictate my relationship with my higher power.

My self-worth and value cannot be taken away by the religious opinions of others.

I am not required to be a member or attend regular services in order to be spiritual.

I have the ability to find harmony with the world around me in a way that suits me.

I am not sinful or shameful for living my truth.

THE CATAGORY IS...

HELPFUL HABITS

It's easy to forget about your well-being, but it's crucial to prioritize your emotional and physical health, especially when life gets busy or overwhelming. The additional challenges you may face as a member of the queer community, such as navigating environments that are not always affirming, can take a toll on you. That's why it's important to pause every once in a while to ensure you're properly taking care of yourself. Make yourself a priority by developing healthy habits, such as setting boundaries, practicing self-care, caring for your health, and keeping a positive mindset. Doing these things could go a long way in enhancing your quality of life!

PRIORITIZING YOU

Hey, when was the last time you stepped back and realized your time and energy were valuable resources you own and control? Sometimes, in an effort to please others or prove our worth, we can overextend ourselves to the point where it hurts our physical or mental health. That's when it's time to stop and put yourself first. **Remember, you're important, too!** If you don't set boundaries, you might exhaust yourself, lose sight of your values or goals, resent commitments or people, or become burned out on things you enjoy. **Step back and evaluate what is best for you.** Don't let anyone make you feel guilty or afraid of offending others, even if you need to say no—just be honest and communicate. It's a form of valuing yourself. Now go on and put yourself first, because you are absolutely worth it!

Saying "NO" is okay! It's a way to value your time, needs, feelings, energy, and identity.

WAYS TO SAY NO

"I can't, but thank you for the offer."
"I don't have the bandwidth right now."
"I have another commitment."
"Sorry, I can't help on this occasion."
"I'm honored you asked me, but I can't."
"Unfortunately, I already have plans."
"No, thank you."
"Maybe another time."

Conversations On PRIORITIZING YOURSELF

NACEY (19)

"I want to have a conversation with my two sisters and my mom about what I'm comfortable with and not comfortable with—openly having those hard convos and setting boundaries with them that doesn't surpass my comfort level."

PERCY (18)

"Taking space when I am able to and learning to recognize my social limits have been really important. It isn't selfish to take time for yourself or to say no to things. Learning that took me a long time. It helps to have headphones in my pocket just in case I need some music to ground me. This might be my ADHD talking, but I've found that having something to fidget with really helps too!"

JACKSON (18)

"I'm autistic, so there's a lot of times where certain things are expected of me but it's either really difficult for me to do them, or I just don't know what to do. Sometimes I have to accept that other people might be uncomfortable with how I'm acting even if I'm acting in a way that's normal for me. I have to just accept that I need to stop trying to appear a different way to them when it can be fruitless and just exhausting."

CONSTANCE (19)

"The whole welcoming-people-in-instead-of-coming-out thing is a great example of how I put myself first. It's so important to protect my peace as a trans person because the world right now is always trying to knock me down. I take back power for myself by choosing who gets to know the real me."

CADENCE (13)

"Putting yourself first is something you need to do, and taking care of others is going to be harder if you can't take care of yourself."

ALIA (17)

"I tend to push myself too much, to stretch myself too thin, and I always say yes, but I have gotten better at saying no to things. You have to be comfortable saying no to things you don't want to do or shouldn't do for your well-being, even if it's a great opportunity if you know that your life is going to become unbalanced."

It's Okay for You to...

Say what's on your mind

Ask for help

Ask someone to respect your pronouns

Do a hobby you enjoy

Set clear boundaries

Address your needs

Choose clothes you're comfortable with

Honor your feelings

Take time for you

Distance yourself from unkind people

Decline an invitation

Take a nap when tired

Be assertive and stand up for yourself

Give yourself compassion

Prioritize self-worth over people-pleasing

Try These ACTIVITIES

1 THE BOUNDARY LIST

Write a list of your boundaries and keep them handy for when you need them. Consider your emotional and physical boundaries, as well as those based on your opinions, beliefs, commitments, and values. Make sure to review them once in a while to keep them updated and fresh in your mind.

2 BLOCK IT AND CLOCK IT

Turn off your phone and step away from all required work and distractions. Set a timer for thirty minutes and do something relaxing or refreshing, like reading, walking, or taking a hot bath. Love it? Add these thirty minutes to your weekly schedule!

3 A VERY MERRY UNBIRTHDAY

Usually we wait to celebrate ourselves until special occasions like our birthday. Today, pull out all the stops and celebrate yourself for no reason other than that you are special and unique. Take the day off. Eat the cake. Wear the crown. You deserve it!

STRONGER TOGETHER

QUEER QUESTIONS

DO YOU FREQUENTLY PUT THE NEEDS OF OTHERS BEFORE YOUR OWN?

ASK YOURSELF

QUEER QUESTIONS

DO YOU FEEL LIKE YOU TAKE ENOUGH TIME FOR YOURSELF? WHAT'S ONE KIND THING YOU COULD DO FOR YOURSELF THIS WEEK?

ASK YOURSELF

QUEER QUESTIONS

DO YOU EVER FIND IT DIFFICULT TO SAY NO? WHY?

ASK YOURSELF

QUEER QUESTIONS

DO YOU FIND YOURSELF REPEATEDLY DOING SOMETHING EVEN THOUGH IT DOESN'T FEEL GOOD? IF SO, WHY?

ASK YOURSELF

CARE TO SHARE?

#ShareQueerCheer

RAINBOW AFFIRMATIONS

My time, needs, feelings, and energy are valuable.

I can articulate my needs, feelings, and boundaries to others without fear or judgment.

I am allowed to say no.

I am allowed to put myself first. It's a wonderful way to show my value, honor my needs, and celebrate all that I am.

I am allowed to do what is best for me even if it upsets other people.

I am deserving of respect, love, and kindness. I shouldn't have to sacrifice my comfort to ease someone else's discomfort.

SELF-CARE

Sometimes, we may be so occupied with one aspect of life that we neglect our personal and social needs, or miss out on opportunities to explore other aspects of life. **It's important to take a step back and assess our needs every once in a while.** Are we giving ourselves enough time to unwind and relax? Are we taking measures to address our physical, emotional, and social needs? By incorporating activities that promote self-care, **we can develop healthy habits that keep us positive**, energized, and lead to a more fulfilled and balanced life.

"HOW YOU TAKE CARE OF YOURSELF IS HOW THE WORLD SEES YOU."
—JONATHAN VAN NESS

Conversations On SELF-CARE

KATIE (14)

"I really like to draw. That's one thing I can do wherever I am. I draw a lot of gay couples and stuff. I like to draw characters that represent how I feel at that moment. It helps me relax a lot."

LIS (17)

"Playing my instrument brings me to a sense of meditation where there's nothing else in the world except these little black notes that I play. I also joined winter guard last year, and it kind of feels like I can just take my anger out on that equipment because it doesn't have feelings."

PARKER (16)

"A lot of people who have struggled with mental health struggle with their self-care, like I had. Knowing a task will take longer and spacing that out or separating things into what I know I can handle in a day helps. That even involves basic things like showering and laundry."

EVAN (18)

"I have a hard time with practicing self-care and it's something I'm working on right now, but I'm a very social person and I thrive when I'm in groups. So if I need to be in a better mood, I normally spend time with my friends."

CHACE (17)

"I absolutely love spending time with cows and horses. I'm a level four rider. That's kind of self-care in the sense that I'm really just doing it for me. I also love really loud dance music and I like to dance a lot. And I feel like that is a kind of self-care."

ELIXIR (16)

"For self-care, I watch anime and listen to music. Sometimes I doodle or put on makeup and vibe for a few hours because that helps me. I find little things I can do easily."

Self-Care Activities

Write a gratitude list	Unplug from social media	Clean your space	Paint your nails
Volunteer	Seek guidance from a mentor	Soak in the tub	Drink a glass of water
Bond with pets or family	Connect with caring queer friends	Dance your heart out	Listen to music or sing
Try breathing exercises	Spend time with people who affirm you	Listen to inspiring queer speakers	Make a therapy appointment
Spend time in nature	Keep a journal	Rest and reflect	Practice affirmations
Read inspirational books	Write a letter (you don't have to send it!)	Do a crossword or puzzle	Plan a dream vacation
Get a makeover	Watch a comedy	Draw or doodle	Set future goals

SELF-CARE 101

Prioritize

- Create a to-do list of home, school, extracurricular activities.
- Rate every task from one to ten based on their priority.
- Prioritize critical tasks that have the biggest impact.
- Consider deadlines and prioritize tasks that are approaching soon.
- Eliminate unnecessary or unwanted tasks if possible.

Create Balance

- Create a weekly schedule with school, home, social and self-care activities.
- Determine if your schedule is realistic, or if you've overcommitted yourself.
- Try scheduling blocks of work, play, and rest, rather than strict schedules.
- Be honest with your time.
- Plan unscheduled time to give yourself a buffer.
- Try using a student planner, calendar, or phone app.

Avoid Procrastination

- Don't put things off until the last minute.
- Break big projects into smaller, more manageable tasks.
- Tackle those tasks sooner rather than later to get ahead.

Learn to say "No"

- If you say yes to everything, you may find yourself juggling more than you can handle.
- Consider your current commitments before accepting new ones.

Stay Healthy

- Eat well, exercise, and get plenty of rest to maintain energy levels.
- Allow time for self-care and social activity.
- Rebalance your priorities if you become exhausted or stressed.
- Take breaks to avoid feeling overwhelmed and stay productive.

1 MEDITATION MODE

Set aside fifteen minutes of your day. Many find it helpful to do this first thing in the morning or right before bed. Sit in a comfortable position and close your eyes. Focus on your breath while clearing your mind or repeating a mantra. This can be an affirmation or a simple word, such as "calm." If your mind wanders, refocus on your breath, or try a guided meditation app. Do this daily and reflect on the practice after a week. Does it help your day?

2 TREAT YOURSELF TO A MINI DIY SPA DAY

A day of pampering can do wonders! Soak your feet, paint your nails, indulge in face masks and body lotion, set up some candles or aromatherapy, or give yourself a hand massage! You can even invite a friend to join!

3 TIME MANAGEMENT TECHNIQUES

There are many different methods and strategies to help you balance your time, such as the Pomodoro Technique, the Pickle Jar Theory, and time blocking. Some have apps or websites to plan with. Research and commit to trying one for a week to find what suits you best!

STRONGER TOGETHER

SELF QUEERY
QUEER QUESTIONS
WHAT IS ONE SELF-CARE HABIT YOU COULD COMMIT TO ADDING TO YOUR DAILY OR WEEKLY ROUTINE?
ASK YOURSELF
QUEER QUESTIONS
WHAT IS ONE THING YOU CAN LET GO OF THAT IS NOT HELPING YOU REACH YOUR GOALS OR MAKING YOU HAPPY?
ASK YOURSELF
QUEER QUESTIONS
HOW COULD YOU CREATE MORE BALANCE IN YOUR LIFE?
ASK YOURSELF
QUEER QUESTIONS
IN WHAT WAYS CAN YOU PRIORITIZE SELF-CARE IN YOUR LIFE?
ASK YOURSELF
CARE TO SHARE?
#ShareQueerCheer

RAINBOW AFFIRMATIONS

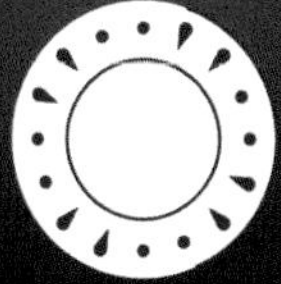

I can say no to adding more things to my plate when my plate is already full.

It's okay to pull out of a commitment if it jeopardizes my mental health.

I can live a harmonious life that balances my time, effort, relationships, and responsibilities.

I am worthy of time spent on joy and fulfillment.

I can reward myself with downtime and rest after working hard to achieve my goals. It's a good way to rebalance.

I can take time to create joy and peace in my life.

NURTURING YOUR BODY

Our bodies are complicated systems made up of muscles, nerves, and organs. They make it possible to **taste a delicious meal, see the beauty in nature, hear the sound of music, feel the touch of a hand, and smell the aroma of a flower**. It's the system that works to keep us alive. That's why it's important to take care of our health. Observing and managing your physical health now will help you feel better. Eating healthier foods, staying active, and getting plenty of sleep are all great ways to stay healthy. If you feel like you need to make changes to better take care of your health, **it might help to start with small actionable steps and aim for healthy changes**, rather than focusing on appearance or weight goals. It can be anything from moving more, to adding more fruit to your meals or keeping a regular sleep schedule. When you take charge of your physical health, you'll find yourself in a better place to tackle whatever comes your way.

REMEMBER...

BODY SHAPES DO NOT TELL YOU ANYTHING ABOUT PEOPLE'S HEALTH.

"GOOD" APPEARANCE DOES NOT EQUATE TO GOOD HEALTH.

ALL OUR INNER WORKINGS NEED POSITIVE CARE.

Conversations On NURTURING YOUR BODY

PERCY (18)

"I'm going to run the risk of sounding like an absolute grandparent here, but I love going to sleep early. I find that I think best in the morning and prioritizing sleep helps me to feel my best. Also, finding physical activities that make me feel good about myself is really important to me. This can be tricky to navigate at times, especially when my gender dysphoria makes it difficult to feel connected to my body in a positive way. Currently, I am loving yoga and Pilates."

JACKSON (18)

"I have some medical issues that make it really difficult to be physically active. I try to take care of my health by understanding my limits and respecting when my body is telling me I can't do something. Yesterday, I didn't try and push myself to go for a walk, which was better for my physical health than if I had tried, but I ended up finding a way to go outside and that was good for my mental health. A couple of years ago, I started recovering from an eating disorder. That's going well, now. Rather than focusing a whole lot on food and the very specific details of nutrition, I try to listen to my body, and if I know I'm not getting enough of a certain thing, I'll add that instead of trying to follow diet culture and restricting myself from eating certain things."

ALIA (17)

"I know someone who recently found out that he was second in our class at school, and he was like, 'All those sleepless nights were worth it,' and I was like, 'I had a lot of nights where I slept, and I thought they were really nice.' I was obviously kind of joking, but I really do think sleep is important. If something is really impressive, but it's going to negatively impact my happiness or health, I'm going to say no to it, because if we are drained, then the work is not going to happen."

NACEY (19)

"Lately, I've been trying to get into working out, not because I'm trying to lose weight, but because I want to help my mental state. I just want to be healthy mentally, and physically is great too, but it's not my priority. When I don't feel like I'm being positive to myself or my body, I try to treat it like a friend. Like I try not to tell it things I wouldn't tell a friend."

IDEAS TO HELP MOTIVATE YOU TOWARD HEALTHY LIVING

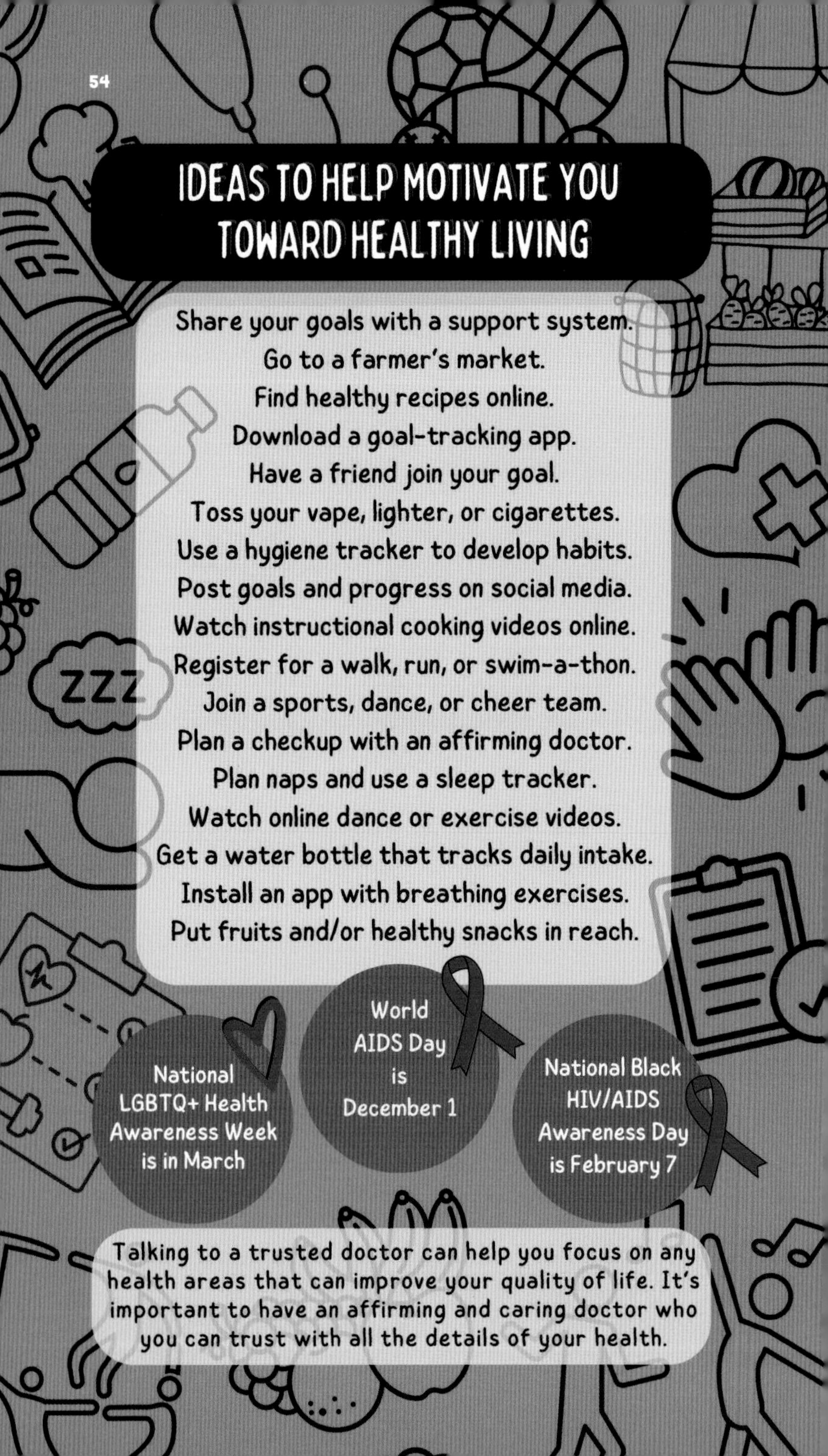

Share your goals with a support system.
Go to a farmer's market.
Find healthy recipes online.
Download a goal-tracking app.
Have a friend join your goal.
Toss your vape, lighter, or cigarettes.
Use a hygiene tracker to develop habits.
Post goals and progress on social media.
Watch instructional cooking videos online.
Register for a walk, run, or swim-a-thon.
Join a sports, dance, or cheer team.
Plan a checkup with an affirming doctor.
Plan naps and use a sleep tracker.
Watch online dance or exercise videos.
Get a water bottle that tracks daily intake.
Install an app with breathing exercises.
Put fruits and/or healthy snacks in reach.

National LGBTQ+ Health Awareness Week is in March

World AIDS Day is December 1

National Black HIV/AIDS Awareness Day is February 7

Talking to a trusted doctor can help you focus on any health areas that can improve your quality of life. It's important to have an affirming and caring doctor who you can trust with all the details of your health.

Try These ACTIVITIES

1 KEEP YOUR SLEEP

Create a bedtime routine and challenge yourself to stick to it for a week! For example, set a consistent bedtime, and make sure to put your phone away at least a half hour before!

2 ADD SOMETHING NEW

Incorporate one new fruit or vegetable into a meal each week.

3 GET HELP

Find a way to add accountability to your physical health goals. Whether it's getting an accountability buddy to join you on daily walks or downloading a fitness app to track your progress and send you reminders, it's easier to meet your goals when you have help along the way.

STRONGER TOGETHER

SELF QUEERY
QUEER QUESTIONS
IN WHAT WAYS CAN YOU OVERCOME ANY BARRIERS OR CHALLENGES TO INCREASE YOUR LEVEL OF PHYSICAL ACTIVITY?
ASK YOURSELF
QUEER QUESTIONS
WHAT IS ONE CHANGE YOU CAN MAKE TO YOUR DAILY ROUTINE THAT WILL HAVE A POSITIVE IMPACT ON YOUR HEALTH?
ASK YOURSELF
QUEER QUESTIONS
HOW CAN YOU MAKE PHYSICAL ACTIVITY MORE ENJOYABLE OR ENGAGING FOR YOURSELF?
ASK YOURSELF
QUEER QUESTIONS
WHAT IS ONE STEP YOU CAN TAKE THIS WEEK TO IMPROVE YOUR EATING HABITS?
ASK YOURSELF
CARE TO SHARE?
#ShareQueerCheer

RAINBOW AFFIRMATIONS

My body deserves to be taken care of.

I have the power to improve my health.

I make choices that nourish and strengthen my body.

My body deserves care and compassion regardless of where I am in my transition journey.

I listen to my body and give myself space to pause and rest when needed.

I can choose physical activities that work for me and my body.

MANAGING EMOTIONS

Life is a mixture of emotions that we often can't control, but we can choose how to respond to them. If you find yourself repressing or ignoring your emotions instead of accepting and responding to them, it may help to take a step back and identify what you're feeling. Taking a deep breath and considering what your feelings might be telling you can go a long way toward accepting them. Then, you can think about how to respond. It may also help to practice self-care or reach for positive affirmations in those tense or emotional moments. Remember, no one is expected to be happy all the time. If you focus on self-care and stress management skills, you will find it easier to evaluate, experience, and manage these feelings. And if the feelings get overwhelming or you're struggling to manage on your own, it's okay to ask for help!

We know our friendly advice is no replacement for professional help. If you're feeling overwhelmed, please reach out to a trusted adult or mental health professional.
If you are in crisis or considering self-harm, please get immediate, 100% free and confidential support at the **Trevor Project; Text "start" to 678-678, Call 866-488-7386 or chat at www.thetrevorproject.org/get-help/**

"THERE IS NOTHING IN NATURE THAT BLOOMS ALL YEAR LONG, SO DON'T EXPECT YOURSELF TO DO SO EITHER." —UNKNOWN

Conversations On MANAGING EMOTIONS

NACEY (19)

"I've gotten better at asking for help. My friend walked me to therapy one time because I couldn't get myself to go. Soon I was going every week, and it was nice, and now I find myself calling crisis when I need help."

ADARA (18)

"I was nervous about asking my parents for therapy because I've never gone through anything traumatic, and I was afraid they would say I didn't need it. I worked up the confidence to ask them by saying I needed to use therapy for an essay. One good thing that came out of it is that I realized that I mask around people, which is sometimes an autism thing and sometimes an ADHD thing."

JACKIE (13)

"If I'm worried about something, meditation can help me clear my mind and focus so I can try to heal it. And I don't really like being angry, so sometimes I listen to certain music or think about certain things to get my anger out. If I'm feeling a certain way, I have people I can go to. I might go to my mom like, 'Hey, I'm struggling,' or I might call a friend and say, 'I need some help.'"

PERCY (18)

"Listening to music helps calm me down. Listening to queer artists can remind us that we're not alone."

LIS (17)

"When I'm having a hard time, I look at myself in the mirror and say, 'It's going to be okay. It's not the end of the world, and I will always love you, no matter what.' Hearing that from myself reminds me that I can always be my own support."

CHACE (17)

"One of my close friends passed away, and that was really difficult for me, along with a group of my peers. It was really challenging for a lot of reasons, and we were able to kind of confide in each other. I don't think that I'd be in the accepting place I am today without a group of people."

KATIE (14)

"My boyfriend has a shirt that says, 'It's okay to not be okay.' I'm obsessed with that quote right now."

PARKER (16)

"My friend and I play characters we created through storylines. It helps us deal with day-to-day struggles because playing as those characters feels like we're living in that story."

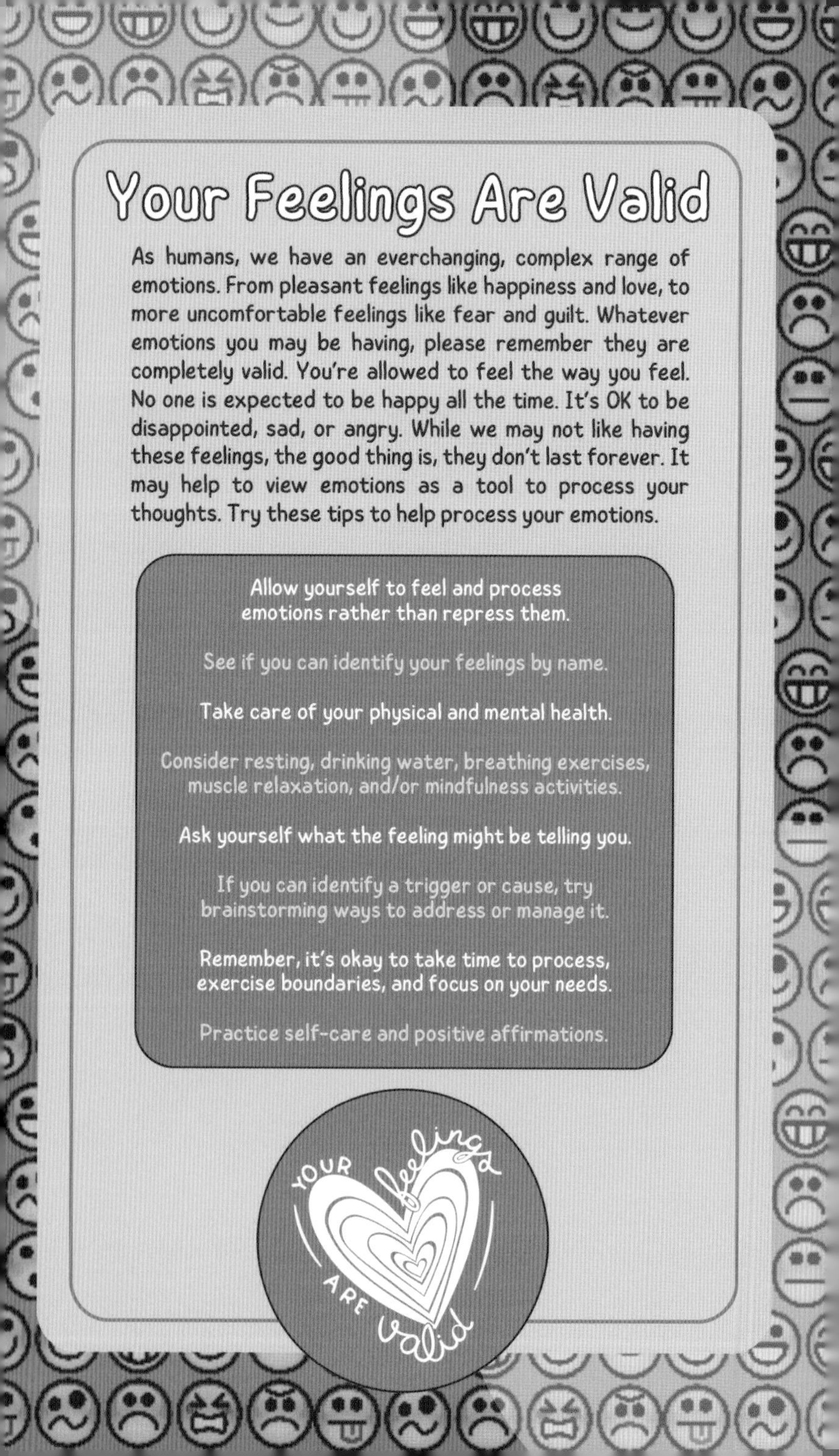

Your Feelings Are Valid

As humans, we have an everchanging, complex range of emotions. From pleasant feelings like happiness and love, to more uncomfortable feelings like fear and guilt. Whatever emotions you may be having, please remember they are completely valid. You're allowed to feel the way you feel. No one is expected to be happy all the time. It's OK to be disappointed, sad, or angry. While we may not like having these feelings, the good thing is, they don't last forever. It may help to view emotions as a tool to process your thoughts. Try these tips to help process your emotions.

Allow yourself to feel and process emotions rather than repress them.

See if you can identify your feelings by name.

Take care of your physical and mental health.

Consider resting, drinking water, breathing exercises, muscle relaxation, and/or mindfulness activities.

Ask yourself what the feeling might be telling you.

If you can identify a trigger or cause, try brainstorming ways to address or manage it.

Remember, it's okay to take time to process, exercise boundaries, and focus on your needs.

Practice self-care and positive affirmations.

WHEN MANAGING DIFFICULT FEELINGS ISN'T WORKING

Sometimes it might be difficult to manage certain situations or feelings on our own, and that's okay! If you're struggling, reach out to someone you trust and ask for help. If you need immediate assistance and can't get the help you need, contact a crisis helpline.

988 Suicide & Crisis Lifeline
988lifeline.org
Text or Call 988

SIGNS YOU MAY NEED TO ASK FOR HELP

- Constantly exhausted/tired
- Constantly angry
- Restless and agitated
- Finding it hard to think clearly
- Feeling trapped/hopeless
- Having mood swings/trouble managing feelings
- Finding it hard to cope with life
- Struggling with grief
- Sad/tearful all the time
- Feeling unsafe or threatened
- Having thoughts of self-harm
- Forced to do things you don't want to
- Afraid at home or at school
- Missing a lot of school
- Avoiding/lost the desire to be around others
- Using alcohol/drugs to cope
- Constantly hungry or lack proper shelter

JACKSON TALKS ABOUT DEALING WITH GENDER DYSPHORIA

"I wouldn't tell anyone that you'll just get better if you don't give up, like it will just magically get better, because honestly, it probably won't. Dysphoria that requires transition to be treated, which is the case for a lot of people, won't just go away if you change your mindset on it. But also, I'd tell them that I'm really glad that I made it through those years where I couldn't medically transition and that I hope they get there too. Because, even if someone has to wait until they turn eighteen, there's the whole rest of our lives where we get to transition as we need to, and we can be comfortable and happy in our bodies and who we are. I was suicidal at several points, definitely largely because I couldn't medically transition, and I've managed to make it through that, and I think it was worth it. I'm really glad that I'm still alive. But I want to acknowledge that it is really, really difficult for a lot of people to make it through those years where they can't medically transition, and that that pain is real and valid. I don't want to tell them, 'Hey, it's okay for now. You'll make it there.' I want to say something like, 'I really hope that you try to, because even if it's really, really bad for a couple of years, which I know can be a long time, everyone deserves to get to that point where they can medically transition, and there's going to be a day where you can. So, try and hold on till then. Because at that point, it really does get better and it'll be worth it.' "

- Jackson

Need someone to talk to?
Call the Trans Lifeline:
(877) 565-8860   translifeline.org/hotline

1 READY REFERENCES

Sometimes it's hard to remember things when you're blue. Make a list to remind you of self-care strategies and keep it somewhere easy to access. On an index card, list three of each: People you trust to talk to. Activities to distract you. People to call who make you laugh. Self-care activities to try (walking, music, shower). Resources for meditations/breathing/mindfulness. Positive affirmations. Contact numbers/websites for help.

2 SOCIAL MEDIA EXPLORATION

Scroll through your different social media sites and notice your mood. How does the content impact you? Try staying offline for a day and see how you feel.

3 MINDFULNESS AND MEDITATION

Mindfulness is a grounding technique that can sometimes help manage anxiety, stress, or depression. Try one of these techniques to see if they help you: 1) With your eyes closed, breathe in and out to the count of four. 2) Rub different textures while describing them. 3) Focus on naming three things in your space you can see, touch, hear, and/or smell.

STRONGER TOGETHER

SELF QUEERY
QUEER QUESTIONS
WHAT HELPS YOU FEEL BETTER WHEN YOU'RE UPSET OR STRESSED?
ASK YOURSELF
QUEER QUESTIONS
WHAT IS ONE THING YOU CAN DO RIGHT NOW TO IMPROVE YOUR SITUATION?
ASK YOURSELF
QUEER QUESTIONS
WHO CAN YOU CALL TO VENT?
ASK YOURSELF
QUEER QUESTIONS
DO YOU STRUGGLE WITH TRYING TO CONTROL THINGS OUTSIDE OF YOUR CONTROL?
ASK YOURSELF
CARE TO SHARE?
#ShareQueerCheer

RAINBOW AFFIRMATIONS

I am still a good person, even if I have trauma or drama to navigate.

I am resourceful. I can always find a way to get help if I need to.

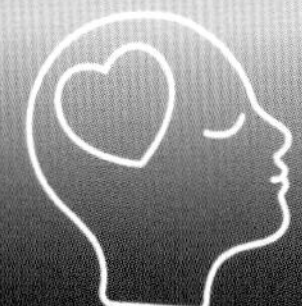

I am worthy and capable of more than my mind tells me I am.

My feelings are information my body sends me, but I get to decide how I use that information.

I will stay hopeful and believe in my ability to weather this storm.

I am strong and proud of myself for getting through difficult times.

CHANGING PERSPECTIVES

Changing your perspective can be a powerful tool in managing difficult situations. While negative events can be challenging, sometimes **you can help reduce the impact they have on your life by shifting your outlook**. Instead of dwelling on the negatives, try finding a perspective that shifts your focus and helps you regain some control of the situation. Perhaps it's the strength of our community, a new opportunity, hope for the future, or the experience you've gained. **There is more than one way to see an experience or event**, and if you look deep enough, you may just find a new perspective that reduces stress, increases confidence, or makes life more manageable.

"THE OPTIMIST SEES THE DONUT:
THE PESSIMIST SEES THE HOLE."
—OSCAR WILDE

Conversations On
CHANGING PERSPECTIVES

LUKE (16)

"I'm a very visual person and I like pulling myself back in situations and looking at the pros and cons. Almost every time you look at the full picture, you really see that there's so many more positives about the situation."

PERCY (18)

"Sometimes you need distance from a moment to look at it in a different way, but also sometimes things just suck and there isn't a silver lining. It's okay to have a negative experience and carry it with you, but it's important not to let that thing stop you from living your life. We can learn to let something stick with us while not letting it hold us back from moving forward and having other positive experiences."

CADENCE (13)

"My cousin makes fun of me and calls me slurs. He has issues. It's not about me, it's all about him. I know he has a tough life, and it's understandable why he does it, but it doesn't make it right. It's really hard when other people don't accept you, especially if you're a people-pleaser, but not everyone is going to accept you and you have to deal with it. I've grown to not care what he thinks. The more you care about what other people think, the less happy you'll be."

SHALOM (18)

"I learned this quote, 'Your story isn't over until you get your happy ending.' And so when bad things happen, I always think about that. I'm like, 'You know what? This is just the low point. We're gonna get out of here. If things are rough for you, then it's gonna look up.' Maybe that's the end of one story, you know, or the beginning of another."

CONSTANCE (19)

"I always think, 'Things won't be this way forever' whenever I see something disheartening in the news or if something happens to me. It can definitely get hard to be optimistic when you're a trans WOC, but I just think about how young I am and how I get to be a part of a generation that really cares about change and fights hard for the underdog."

TIPS TO CHANGE YOUR MIND FRAME

- Avoid gossip
- Practice self-care
- Talk it over
- Smile!
- Write three things you're grateful for each morning
- Throughout your day, look for small things to appreciate
- Celebrate when good things happen
- Practice positive self-talk
- Practice living in the moment; put away your phone, focus on how you feel
- Use affirmations each day
- Replace sources of negativity (music, media, news, websites, social media, people!)
- Focus on the good things (no matter how small!)
- Do something nice for someone
- Surround yourself with positive people

Reframe Your Thoughts

INSTEAD OF	TRY THINKING
I can't do it.	I can't do it...yet!
I'm flawed.	I'm perfectly imperfect.
I have to.	I'm able to.
I'm not good at this.	What am I missing?
I can't cope.	How can I manage this?
I give up.	I'll try a different way.
It's good enough.	Is this really my best?
I am not enough.	I am doing my best.
This is too hard.	The effort is worth it!
I made a mistake.	Mistakes help me learn.
I just can't do this.	I can train my brain.
I'll never be that smart.	I will learn to do this.
Plan A didn't work.	There is always a plan B.
Others are better than me.	I will learn from them.

1 CHANGE YOUR ENVIRONMENT

Sometimes, in order to change your perspective, you need to change the people, places, or things around you. For example, if all your friends complain about school (boring classes, mean teachers, etc.), you might have negative thoughts about school, too. If all your friends like school (time to socialize with friends, they enjoy the challenge, etc.), you might find yourself enjoying school, too. If you want to change your perspective about something, try evaluating the things around you to see if changing one would help.

2 PLAY PRETEND

Take a situation you're struggling with and write a story or journal entry from the perspective of someone with the opposite viewpoint. Dig deep. What facts or feelings would they express? When you're done, reflect on whether it's made you feel differently about things.

3 TIP THE SCALES

It's so easy for us to focus on negative things in life, and this can sometimes cause us to forget about the various positive things that surround us. If you notice this happening, try tipping the scales. Whenever you find yourself complaining about something, say two positive things related to that issue. Doing this consistently over time can help rewire your brain to focus on the positive things in life.

STRONGER TOGETHER

QUEER QUESTIONS

HOW OFTEN DO YOU FIND YOURSELF FOCUSING ON THE NEGATIVE OR POSITIVE ASPECTS OF A SITUATION?

ASK YOURSELF

QUEER QUESTIONS

THINK ABOUT SOMETHING THAT IS CHALLENGING OR BOTHERING YOU. HAVE YOU TRIED LOOKING AT IT FROM ANOTHER PERSPECTIVE?

ASK YOURSELF

QUEER QUESTIONS

WHAT WAS THE "BEST" MISTAKE YOU'VE EVER MADE?

ASK YOURSELF

QUEER QUESTIONS

THINK BACK TO A TIME WHEN SOMETHING BAD HAPPENED OR SOMETHING DIDN'T QUITE GO THE WAY YOU PLANNED. IS THERE SOMETHING POSITIVE OR BENEFICIAL THAT CAME OUT OF IT?

ASK YOURSELF

CARE TO SHARE?

#ShareQueerCheer

RAINBOW AFFIRMATIONS

I choose to focus on what I can control instead of the things I can't.

I can replace negative thoughts with positive and constructive ones.

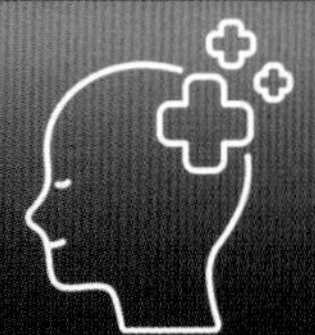

I open my mind to new possibilities instead of focusing on the things I don't have.

I can shift my thinking away from worry and embrace hope instead.

I am smart and can find creative solutions to problems when I step back and look at things another way.

I can explore perspectives that give events new meaning and opportunity.

THE CATAGORY IS... CONFIDENCE

Confidence isn't something you're just born with. It's something you build. It's true! Anyone can build confidence with enough patience and practice, and once you've built it, you'll notice an increase in the way you perceive yourself because self-confidence can contribute greatly to one's self-esteem. A boost in both can make life a little easier, because you'll start being your own best advocate. It starts with believing that you deserve to be here and you deserve good things. Trust us, you do!

BELIEVING IN YOURSELF

While confidence is something you can practice slipping on like a fancy coat that you show off as you strut down the runway, believing in yourself is something deep down inside—the conviction that you know your own worth. **Don't let fear, negative stereotypes, past failures, or the words of anyone else stop you from recognizing the tremendous value you have in this world.** In fact, everyone has unique skills, strengths, and attributes that make them valuable. It's true! There are things about you that people love, so why not take the time to examine those things and learn to love them too?! Start overcoming self-doubt by realizing life is about learning from our mistakes, accepting our flaws, celebrating what makes us special, and staying positive. Don't let outside opinions or people dictate what you can or cannot do; all that matters is that you believe in yourself! **You are fabulous, and can do whatever you put your mind to.** After all, when you believe in yourself, it's a whole lot easier to strut that confidence!

"REMEMBER WHAT THINGS MAKE YOU SPECIAL AND EMBRACE THOSE, BECAUSE THERE ARE SO MANY THINGS THAT AREN'T ON THE OUTSIDE THAT ARE SO IMPORTANT."
—MILEY CYRUS

Conversations On
BELIEVING IN YOURSELF

ALIA (17)

"I heard something about a lot of marginalized people being less likely to apply for a job if they are missing any of the qualifications, whereas cis straight white men are like, 'Whatever, I'll just apply.' Sometimes, people have been told they are not enough, and they believe it, but you might as well try because someone else might get the job because they have unearned confidence."

LIS (17)

"It doesn't really matter what other people think if you don't believe it yourself. A compliment is only as good as what you believe it to be."

NACEY (19)

"I am reaffirming myself every day. 'You can do this. You're smart enough. You're not stupid.' Especially when starting a new job. I know I'm going to suck at it at first, but I know I can do it. I'm capable. Having that trust with myself and not comparing myself to other people's expectations is huge."

JACKIE (13)

"Take the downsides that you see in things and make them your upsides. So, if you have a weakness, turn it into your strength. If you have a lack of confidence about something, try not to focus on the things that are not going well. Instead, focus on the things that are going well."

CADENCE (13)

"I'm a theater kid, so I've learned to act confident if I need to be, even when I'm not. What I've come to realize is that the more you accept yourself for who you are, the more confident you will become."

EVAN (18)

"My boyfriend gives me confidence for everything. If I'm feeling like something will go wrong, he helps me see things from a different angle and shows the positive side. He lifts me up and helps push me through difficult times. He's my biggest hype man."

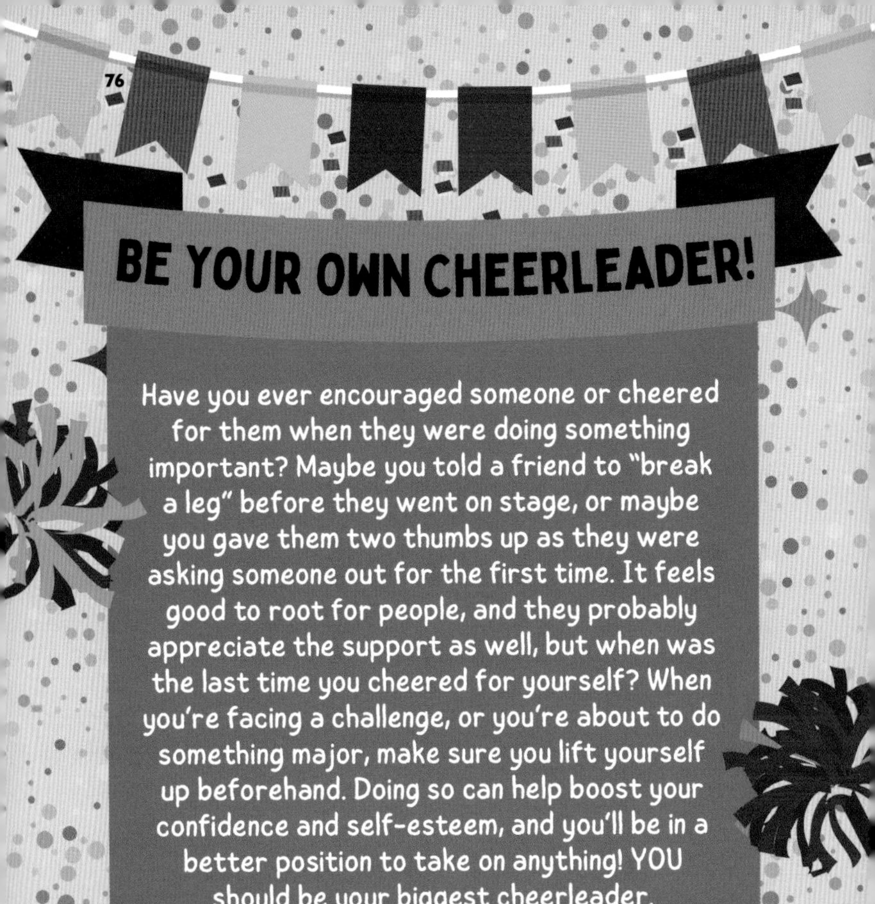

BE YOUR OWN CHEERLEADER!

Have you ever encouraged someone or cheered for them when they were doing something important? Maybe you told a friend to "break a leg" before they went on stage, or maybe you gave them two thumbs up as they were asking someone out for the first time. It feels good to root for people, and they probably appreciate the support as well, but when was the last time you cheered for yourself? When you're facing a challenge, or you're about to do something major, make sure you lift yourself up beforehand. Doing so can help boost your confidence and self-esteem, and you'll be in a better position to take on anything! YOU should be your biggest cheerleader.

1, 2, 3, 4
KICK THAT DOUBT RIGHT OUT THE DOOR!
5, 6, 7, 8
DON'T FORGET THAT
YOU ARE GREAT!
IF YOUR FEAR STARTS TO DECEIVE,
CHEER AGAIN TILL YOU BELIEVE!

BE YOUR OWN CHEERLEADER!

GIVE YOURSELF CREDIT

MAKE A CHEER TO CELEBRATE YOU

FORM AN ALLIANCE (SQUAD) TO CHEER YOU ON

DECORATE A WALL WITH YOUR ACCOMPLISHMENTS

ENCOURAGE YOURSELF

PRACTICE POWER POSES

COMPLIMENT YOURSELF

LIST YOUR POSITIVE QUALITIES

BOOST CONFIDENCE BY SHARING KNOWLEDGE

Sharing what you know and what you're good at can boost your self-esteem and make you feel more empowered. Here are some suggestions to get started, or you can explore ideas that align with your unique strengths!

Start a social media account reviewing your favorite movies, TV shows, or books.

Start a gaming group and teach your favorite board games.

Tutor a math student at your school.

Lead a book club with your favorite book genre.

Share queer icons at your GSA.

Teach about queer history in your history class.

Lead a dance class at your local gym.

Teach friends how to make your favorite recipes.

1 COVER OF CHEER

Create a textbook cover with a paper bag. It's easy to find instructions online. When finished, decorate it with things you love. Doodle on it, or cut out pictures from magazines and glue them on. Don't forget to add affirmations, positive words, and a few rainbows! Boost your confidence for difficult subjects with positive self-notes! Examples of strengths: empathetic, team player, spontaneous, adaptable, resilient, and planner.

2 PUMP ME UP POSTER

Make a list of your strengths, accomplishments, and talents. Find the words in a magazine, or print them from a computer and arrange them on a poster board. Display it on your wall.

3 CREATE YOUR OWN ELEVATOR PITCH

Think of something you want, like a party during pride month, a later curfew, votes for class president, etc. Then write down why you want and deserve this, highlighting your recent achievements, talents, skills, positive qualities, and reasons your ask is beneficial. Combine these into a memorized one-minute speech and practice delivering it clearly until you feel confident.

SELF QUEERY
QUEER QUESTIONS
IN WHAT AREAS OF YOUR LIFE ARE YOU MOST CRITICAL OF YOURSELF? IN WHAT AREAS DO YOU BELIEVE IN YOURSELF?
ASK YOURSELF
QUEER QUESTIONS
WHAT ARE THE BEST COMPLIMENTS YOU'VE EVER RECEIVED?
ASK YOURSELF
QUEER QUESTIONS
IN WHICH SITUATIONS DO YOU COMPARE YOURSELF TO OTHERS?
QUEER QUESTIONS
WHEN YOU FEEL DISCOURAGED, WHAT ARE SOME WORDS YOU COULD TELL YOURSELF?
ASK YOURSELF
CARE TO SHARE?
#ShareQueerCheer

RAINBOW AFFIRMATIONS

I will hold my head high and invest in my self-esteem.

I can make decisions with confidence.

It's okay not to know everything.

I am worthy.

I can do this. I believe in myself.

I am proud of who I am.

BODY IMAGE

Body positivity is for everyone! All bodies are unique, and they have value regardless of their shape, size, color, abilities, or gender. Our bodies work hard for us, and they deserve care, respect, and compassion. Society has created an unrealistic standard of beauty and gender in regard to what people should wear, how much they should weigh, and so much more, but **beauty is determined by you**, not the images highlighted in movies, TV shows, commercials, magazines, or on social media. Instead of focusing on what your body looks like, try to focus on what your body can do for you, or how it serves you. You have the right to cherish your body and live in it in a way that is right for you, honoring your unique needs and experiences. So, eat that pizza or eat that salad. Wear that dress, tux, tube top, or binder! Shave your head, or let your hair grow! Do whatever the hell you want, because **your body is your body**, and when you focus more on what makes you look good and feel good about yourself, rather than the expectations other people have for you, your confidence will soar. Be who you are and be proud of it! Remember, your body is the space you deserve to take in this world!

BE YOUR OWN BFF

THINK ABOUT YOUR BFF OR SOMEONE YOU LOVE. DO YOU FOCUS ON THEIR PHYSICAL IMPERFECTIONS? DOES THEIR APPEARANCE PREVENT YOU FROM LOVING THEM?

NOPE!

NOW TREAT YOURSELF AS YOUR OWN BEST FRIEND!

Conversations On BODY IMAGE

CADENCE (13)

"I'm still trying to figure out my look. Popular clothing styles are constantly changing and how I present myself is definitely related to my mood and how I feel at the time. I used to have my hair long and then I cut it short. I'm still trying to figure out what I like best. I'm always going to try new things."

ZIE (17)

"When I started interacting on the internet, I didn't want to use my gender at the time, so I just used they/them pronouns and hid the fact that I was a woman for safety, and I liked that so much more than she/her. I realized what I felt about my body was actually dysphoria and I was like, 'OMG! The pieces are coming together!' "

ALIA (17)

"For a while, I wore a binder almost every day, and I think I was doing that for other people's perception of me. Now, I wear it sometimes, but that's when I want to. I also never used to wear pink. I didn't like the color because of the expectation that girls were supposed to like it. But looking back, I didn't actually hate pink. I just hated that expectation of me. So, now I'm being more true to myself, and doing things because I want to, rather than doing things because I'm being told to."

ELIXIR (16)

"Get friends that hype you up. All my body confidence has come from my friends. We give each other compliments. 'You look great in your clothes. That hairstyle really suits you.' That's how I have better body positivity. We find something we like about the person and we compliment them on that."

JACKIE (13)

"Not that long ago, I was having self-doubts about the way I looked, so I reached out to a friend, and they were super kind and reassuring. It made me feel a lot better."

JACKSON (18)

"I came out as trans, but had an eating disorder, and hated my body. At some point I realized that, even if it didn't really match with who I was as a person, hating my body wasn't going to help, and the things that needed a transition to fix weren't just going to disappear if I tried to lose weight. Then I was able to start manually transitioning. When I turned eighteen, I no longer had to rely on my family for medically necessary care, and then I became a lot more confident in my own body."

CALLAHAN (18)

"I have a metabolic disorder, so I've been overweight for most of life, but I don't really struggle with being overweight anymore. Who I am as a person is not tied to this body. Being trans, though, is something I struggle with. Having boobs is a huge thing for me. I wear a binder all the time, and clothes are a huge thing that help me. My girlfriend and my friends have really helped affirm that not having certain parts does not make me less of a man or less of a partner."

FIVE THINGS TO DO WHEN YOU'RE NOT FEELING GOOD ABOUT YOUR BODY

1. Wear comfortable clothes.
2. Avoid triggers like social media.
3. Treat yourself with compassion.
4. Remind yourself of the progress you've made.
5. Say an affirmation from this book or one you've created on your own.

MY BODY IS THE HOUSE MY BRAIN LIVES IN. I CAN DECORATE IT THE WAY I WANT AND MAKE IT COZY FOR ITS MOST IMPORTANT GUEST: ME!

1 SOCIAL MEDIA EDIT

Social media accounts are constantly bombarded with images of what society thinks is "perfect," but remember, algorithms push things out to our feeds based on past behavior, so train them to push positivity your way. Follow accounts that highlight all kinds of bodies and make sure you interact with them via likes, shares, and comments. Also, consider unfollowing accounts that give you negative feelings.

2 THE COMPLIMENT COUNTDOWN

Set a timer for ninety seconds. Stand in front of a mirror and compliment different things about what you see until the timer goes off. Repeat this every day for one week and reevaluate how you feel about yourself.

3 A NEW IMAGE

Experiment with your look. Attempt a new hairstyle. Try on a new outfit. Paint your nails. Put on makeup. Try a binder or gender-affirming clothing. Maybe experiment with gender expressions and styles. We're not saying to change who you are. Instead, we're saying it's sometimes fun to experiment with your image, and you might just find out something new about yourself.

STRONGER TOGETHER

SELF QUEERY
QUEER QUESTIONS
WHAT IS ONE THING YOU CAN DO TODAY TO FEEL MORE COMFORTABLE IN YOUR OWN SKIN?
ASK YOURSELF
QUEER QUESTIONS
HOW DO YOU CURRENTLY SHOW YOUR BODY RESPECT? WHAT OTHER WAYS CAN YOU SHOW YOUR BODY RESPECT?
ASK YOURSELF
QUEER QUESTIONS
WHAT IS ONE THING ABOUT YOUR BODY THAT YOU LOVE AND WHY?
ASK YOURSELF
QUEER QUESTIONS
HOW DO YOU FEEL ABOUT YOUR BODY? HOW MUCH DOES THE OPINION OF OTHERS INFLUENCE THAT?
ASK YOURSELF
CARE TO SHARE?
#ShareQueerCheer

RAINBOW AFFIRMATIONS

I will not let other people's opinions of my body affect my self-value.

My body has value even if it isn't exactly what I want it to be.

I do not need to meet anyone else's body standards.

My gender is valid regardless of where I am with my medical transition process.

My relationship and comfort level with my body is allowed to fluctuate.

My worth doesn't depend on how I look, how much I weigh, or how many muscles I have.

GETTING IN THE ZONE

Have you ever experienced those fluttering feelings in your stomach, sweaty palms, or a mix of nervous and excited emotions before a big event? Maybe it was an end-of-year test, trying out for the swim team, coming out to your parents, or going on a first date. Regardless of the event, **preparing yourself mentally and emotionally can help you feel comfortable and confident.** So take a moment to "get in the zone" and set yourself up for success! You've got this!

"WHEN I DARE TO BE POWERFUL —TO USE MY STRENGTH IN THE SERVICE OF MY VISION—THEN IT BECOMES LESS AND LESS IMPORTANT WHETHER I AM AFRAID."
—AUDRE LORDE

Conversations On GETTING IN THE ZONE

CONSTANCE (19)

"When preparing for a big event, I don't think my routine is too different from that of a cis girl. I get ready, do my makeup, and listen to my favorite songs as I drive there. When I was thirteen, my mom taught me to say, "I'm confident, I'm capable, and I'm in control of my emotions" whenever I felt like any of those things wasn't true. I still do it to this day when I feel insecure."

PERCY (18)

"If I'm nervous for a conversation, I prepare myself by writing down all my thoughts. Even if it's something I'm not going to say, it helps to write everything down and get it all out. Sometimes it helps to have something with you that gives you comfort. I like wearing my ring that I can fidget with. If you're into crystals, bring them with you, or maybe wear a comfy sweatshirt so it feels like a hug. Sometimes we just need a little thing that can ground us in a situation that feels scary."

SHALOM (18)

"I listen to a lot of house music. I listen to Beyonce. I'll listen to Charlie XCX. I'll just listen to music that makes me feel good. You know what I mean? And I'll text my friends. I try to engage in things that make me feel good while also communicating with people that reinforce those positive feelings so that I can go back to where I need to be."

LUCY (19)

"Honestly, the biggest thing that I think has made nervous events more manageable for me is just like not thinking about them at all."

WAYS TO HELP GET IN THE ZONE

HAVE LOVED ONES AND FRIENDS LIFT YOU UP AND SUPPORT YOU.

LISTEN TO HIGH-ENERGY MUSIC.

PRACTICE DAILY AFFIRMATIONS RELATED TO THE EVENT.

RESEARCH THE EVENT.

BRING SOMETHING FROM A LOVED ONE.

LOOK UP SOME STRONG ROLE MODELS FOR INSPIRATION.

SAY A PRAYER, MEDITATE, OR MAKE A WISH.

LIST PAST ACHIEVEMENTS TO REMIND YOURSELF OF HOW FAR YOU'VE COME.

MAKE A GOOD LUCK CHARM OR CREATE A GOOD LUCK RITUAL.

Make sure you are in tip-top condition before an event by getting proper rest and a good meal.

1 GOOD LUCK CHARMS

Four-leaf clovers, horseshoes, and even pennies have been rumored to bring good luck if you can find them, but we can make our own good fortune as well! Look up instructions on how to make a good luck charm, such as the three keys, a paper scroll, or other item. You can even find a special piece of jewelry to wear and make a wish on it if you're short on time.

2 GHOST TEXT

Schedule a text to yourself, or a pop-up reminder, that you'll receive right before the event, pumping yourself up with positive affirmations and reasons why it will go great!

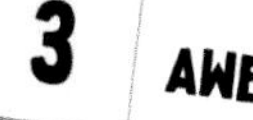

3 AWESOME ANTHEMS

Make a playlist of songs that get you in the zone. These could be fast-paced tunes that get you dancing with excitement, or power ballads that have you belting out your desires. Whatever you choose, make sure the songs pump you up for whatever big things are coming your way.

STRONGER TOGETHER

SELF QUEERY
QUEER QUESTIONS
DO YOU HAVE A SPECIFIC MANTRA YOU LIVE BY? IF SO, WHAT IS IT?
ASK YOURSELF
QUEER QUESTIONS
WHAT IS SOMETHING YOU CAN DO TO BETTER PREPARE YOURSELF FOR A CHALLENGE YOU'RE FACING?
QUEER QUESTIONS
WHAT MAKES YOU FEEL STRONGER?
ASK YOURSELF
QUEER QUESTIONS
THINK ABOUT A TOUGH SITUATION IN THE PAST. WHAT COULD HAVE HELPED YOU BETTER PREPARE FOR IT?
ASK YOURSELF
CARE TO SHARE?
#ShareQueerCheer

RAINBOW AFFIRMATIONS

Today is going to be a good day because I'm going to make it a good day.

I will accomplish everything I need to do today.

I am in the right place, at the right time, and ready to rock.

I have everything I need to achieve my goals.

I am adaptable and can take on anything that comes my way.

I am organized. I am focused. I can do this!

STEPPING OUT

When you stay in your lane for too long, you may miss out on valuable opportunities for growth and progress. Stepping out of the familiar and predictable may come with some nerves, but the benefits are worth it! **By pushing yourself to try new things, you can gain new skills, find untapped strengths, and learn a lot about yourself and the world around you.** Whether it's giving a speech in your class, taking a driver's test, organizing a protest, or trying out drag for the first time, stepping out of your comfort zone can help you learn who you are and what you're really capable of. Even if you don't slay it on the first try, these experiences can help you learn and grow. By taking safe risks and embracing your curiosity, you can level up, build your confidence, and transform into the ultimate version of yourself!

"IT TAKES COURAGE TO GROW UP AND BECOME WHO YOU REALLY ARE."
—E. E. CUMMINGS

Conversations On STEPPING OUT

CHACE (17)

"There was a girl who had a backpack and my friend wanted to know where she got it from, but they were too scared to ask. I was like, okay, I could either go ask and have the possibility of embarrassing myself, or not and I might regret not being able to do this nice thing for my friend. I made the decision to ask, and it ended up going really great. I now have this person's phone number and we're gonna hang out. That's something that never would have happened if I didn't take a chance."

ALIA (17)

"Sometimes, it seems like I'm in control of the situation, but in reality, I have no idea what I'm doing. I'm just pretending I do. One time, I was invited to the governor's office, and people were coming in and I was just talking to them as if I knew how to act in that scenario, but I didn't. I was just faking it, and now I have all these great contacts. I was like, 'Yes, I'd love to speak at this press conference,' because I convinced myself I could. You can't learn anything without trying, so you might as well try."

PERCY (18)

"I performed at an open mic night, and it was nerve-racking because I didn't know most of the people there. I ended up going with a group of friends, and having a small community of people I already knew and loved by my side while doing something scary in a larger social setting was amazing. I ended up having an amazing time and am planning on continuing to perform at open mics in the future."

EVAN (18)

"I decided to let my cousin paint my nails and do my makeup. She wound up giving me a full-on makeover; wigs, dresses, makeup, the whole drag experience. All of it in less than half an hour. Did I look good in the end? No...but I still loved it. It was the first time I had ever stepped out of my comfort zone to be more feminine, and I got to explore a side of me that I never knew existed. It was fabulous."

NACEY (19)

"I put in for a single room at college because of my disability of depression. I was an introvert, but after high school, I thought I wanted to live with people because it would help. It was a good thing. I love roommates now and I don't think I could ever live alone."

LOOKING FOR WAYS TO STEP OUTSIDE OF YOUR COMFORT ZONE? SEE IF THESE INTEREST YOU.

- ENROLL IN A CHALLENGING CLASS
- SING IN PUBLIC
- TRY A NEW SPORT OR ACTIVITY
- TRY GOING A DAY WITH NO TECH
- TAKE AN IMPROV CLASS
- TRY A NEW FOOD
- TRY A NEW STYLE
- VOLUNTEER WITH A NONPROFIT OR CHARITY
- ASK YOUR CRUSH ON A DATE
- AUDITION FOR A TALENT SHOW
- MAKE FRIENDS OUTSIDE YOUR CLIQUE

Step Out!

Try These ACTIVITIES

1 FEAR LIST

Get together with your friends and have each of you create a list of things you'd do if you had no fear or reservations. For example, maybe you'd skydive or hang-glide, but you have a fear of heights, or maybe you'd explore caves, but you're claustrophobic. See if there's an activity on someone's list that you could all do together, safely. Try helping each other with baby steps.

2 GET ON STAGE

Do an activity that puts you in front of a crowd. Maybe try singing karaoke, doing comedy on stage, trying out for a school play, or participating in a poetry slam.

3 TAKE YOURSELF ON A DATE

Some activities are commonly done on a date or with a friend, but can you find the confidence to do some of them on your own? Try going to a restaurant and eating at a table by yourself or going to a movie theater by yourself. Make it a regular occurrence, like once a week, until you are comfortable doing so without reservations.

STRONGER TOGETHER

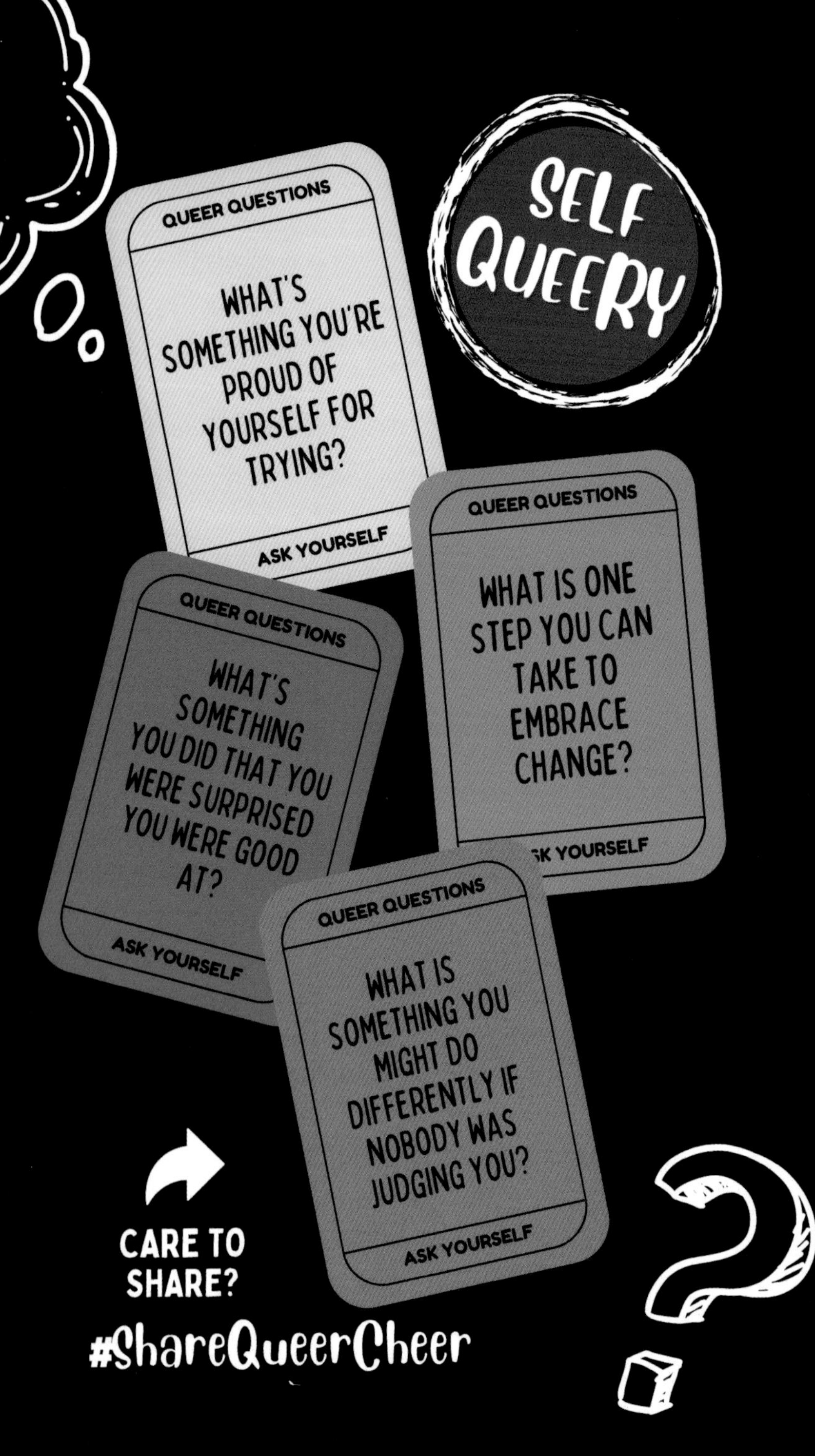
SELF QUEERY
QUEER QUESTIONS
WHAT'S SOMETHING YOU'RE PROUD OF YOURSELF FOR TRYING?
ASK YOURSELF
QUEER QUESTIONS
WHAT'S SOMETHING YOU DID THAT YOU WERE SURPRISED YOU WERE GOOD AT?
ASK YOURSELF
QUEER QUESTIONS
WHAT IS ONE STEP YOU CAN TAKE TO EMBRACE CHANGE?
ASK YOURSELF
QUEER QUESTIONS
WHAT IS SOMETHING YOU MIGHT DO DIFFERENTLY IF NOBODY WAS JUDGING YOU?
ASK YOURSELF
CARE TO SHARE?
#ShareQueerCheer

RAINBOW AFFIRMATIONS

I will not let fear hold me back from a beautiful life.

I am excited to explore new possibilities.

Today I have the courage to step into the unknown.

I focus on the destination when the journey is hard.

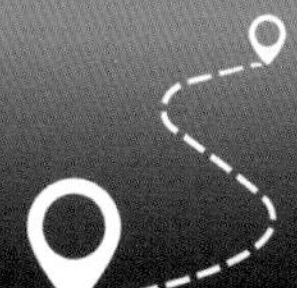

I am open to trying new things.

I am strong. I have done hard things before and I can do them again.

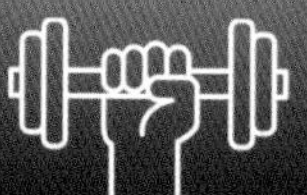

THE CATAGORY IS...

RELATIONSHIPS

Human beings are instinctively drawn to each other, and cultivating positive relationships is a wonderful journey that can lead to fabulous memories and experiences. Relationships form at many levels and in many ways throughout our lives. Some are easy and click right off the bat. Others are hard, and require lots of work. Some are fleeting, and others endure. Navigating these relationships can be both challenging and rewarding, and while we can't always control our relationship experiences, we all get to choose the amount of effort we put into their success.

HEALTHY RELATIONSHIPS

Your day-to-day interactions build relationships with people, from casual acquaintances, like the barista who serves your iced vanilla latte, to more intimate relationships, like your BFFs, partners, and family members.

The nature of your interaction and level of vulnerability will vary depending on the relationship, but all relationships should be healthy and respectful. When you surround yourself with people who accept, appreciate, and respect you, it makes your life so much better. Take time to build trust and communicate boundaries and expectations with quality people. You may want to keep an eye out for red flags and weed out relationships that stress you out rather than lift you up. Sharing personal details about yourself can be scary; it can also lead to some pretty sweet possibilities. After all, the people we choose to share our time with should bring us joy, laughter, and love, and make life absolutely fabulous!

"A HEALTHY RELATIONSHIP IS ONE THAT OFFERS ME SUPPORT AND HELPS ME GROW."
—UNKNOWN

Conversations On RELATIONSHIPS

JACKSON (18)

"Honesty is important to me. I want to be able to trust that people are telling the truth and not have to worry about whether or not they really mean what they say. There's this expression that says, 'True friends stab you in the front, not in the back.' Being up front is something that I value in people in general, especially with people I'm close to."

PARKER (16)

"It's important to me to have people love me for who I am. My mom wanted to keep me as her daughter, but at a certain point, I needed to transition and be who I wanted to be and not what she wanted."

NACEY (19)

"I think I really want to surround myself in healthy relationships. That's my most important goal. Setting my boundaries—not just respecting myself, but others respecting them—and having better relationships with people."

CONSTANCE (19)

"Focus on letting people who matter in, as opposed to sharing yourself with anyone who will hear it."

JACKIE (13)

"Trust is one of the most important things to me. If you have a trustworthy friend, you can be open with them about anything. Like, if you tell them a secret or if you come out to them and don't want anyone else to know just yet, you don't have to worry about them spilling out information."

IS YOUR RELATIONSHIP A HEALTHY ONE?

GREEN FLAGS	RED FLAGS
Honest	Compares you to others
Trustworthy	Brings unhappiness or unease
Dependable	Gossips about you
Respects your boundaries	Betrays your confidence
Open communication	Puts you down or insults you
Respects your independence	Often absent when needed
Lets you make decisions, too	Focuses only on their problems
Accepts you	Puts less effort in relationship
Prioritizes kindness	Drains your energy
Forgives mistakes	Doesn't reciprocate listening
Appreciates you	Disregards your pronouns or name
Is willing to be vulnerable	Shames your sexual orientation
Tries to understand you	Doesn't honor your gender
Doesn't judge you	Betrays your trust
Has your back	Tries to control you
Empowers you	Uses violence, coercion, or force
Celebrates your queer identities	Engages in gaslighting

1 THE PROJECT PLANNERS

Decide on a project and plan it together. It can be planting a garden, making a piece of art, choreographing a dance routine, or something else entirely. Just make it something you'll both enjoy. You'll learn a lot about how you work together. Communicating and compromising will make the project easier.

2 THE COMPLIMENT GAME

Challenge each other to give one compliment every day for a week. Observe how your mood changes during the week and how your relationships are impacted. Afterwards, reflect and determine whether it helped to strengthen your bonds.

3 ABUNDANCE OF APPRECIATION

Find someone you want to have a better relationship with. It could be a single person or a group. Spend a week noting all the things you appreciate about the other person/people and write them down on a list. Have them do the same for you. At the end of the week, exchange lists.

STRONGER TOGETHER

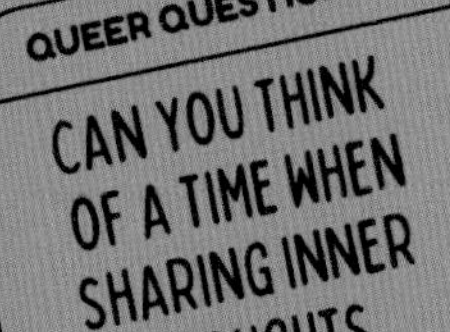

QUEER QUESTIONS

CAN YOU THINK OF A TIME WHEN SHARING INNER THOUGHTS BROUGHT YOU CLOSER TO SOMEONE?

ASK YOURSELF

QUEER QUESTIONS

WHAT DO YOU LOOK FOR IN THE VARIOUS TYPES OF RELATIONSHIPS YOU HAVE (FRIEND, FAMILY, ROMANTIC)?

ASK YOURSELF

QUEER QUESTIONS

DO YOU THINK PEOPLE CAN CHANGE? WHY OR WHY NOT?

ASK YOURSELF

QUEER QUESTIONS

ARE THERE ANY RELATIONSHIPS IN YOUR LIFE WITH TOO MANY RED FLAGS? IF SO, WHAT CAN YOU DO ABOUT THEM?

ASK YOURSELF

CARE TO SHARE?

#ShareQueerCheer

RAINBOW AFFIRMATIONS

I deserve to be treated with respect and dignity at all times.

I am allowed to acknowledge my shame or guilt and still be a good person.

I deserve love and kindness.

I have the strength and self-respect to remove myself from unhealthy relationships.

It's okay to protect myself and hold back if it doesn't feel safe to share.

I can choose not to respond to negative people and to protect my peace.

BEING ACCEPTED FOR YOU

We all want to be accepted by the people we care about, especially when we're living our truth and sharing all that makes us unique. But that acceptance is beyond our control—all you can do is be true to yourself, and if someone doesn't like it, that's their problem, not yours. It can be a real struggle when you're not embraced with open arms, but **it's important to focus on what makes you fabulous and surround yourself with folks who celebrate every inch of your incredible self.** You are deserving of all the love and respect in the world! Don't waste your time and energy on people who can't see how truly amazing you are. Remember, while it's great to feel validated by others, **the most important thing is that you accept and celebrate yourself**, because you are the only one who can truly define who you are, and you are beyond amazing!

REMEMBER...

FITTING IN IS BEING SOMEONE ELSE. BELONGING IS BEING ACCEPTED FOR BEING YOU!

Conversations On BEING ACCEPTED

CADENCE (13)

"It's really hard when other people don't accept you, especially if you're a people pleaser, but not everyone is going to accept you and you have to deal with it. The more you accept yourself, and don't care what other people think of you, the more you will be happy with the person you are."

PERCY (18)

"Feeling like you're able to be your full self around someone, and being able to work through issues when you come to them, is important. Like, if someone doesn't fully understand you or your pronouns or names, knowing they want to understand is important. If someone is not supportive, knowing it's okay to step back and meet them halfway is okay, too."

CHACE (17)

"Sometimes I'm with one of my friends who somebody assumes is LGBTQ+ and they don't assume I am, and they treat us differently. And that's something that I'm still trying to work through. It's a unifying experience that maybe I don't have because I don't look or express myself a certain way. But that's not something that I look to change because I'm very happy with the way that I look and express myself."

PARKER (16)

"My dad clicked with my name right away, but it took longer for my pronouns. My grandma took a little longer to get used to my name and stuff. My grandpa was a different story; he didn't start using my name or pronouns until about a year ago."

ELIXIR (16)

"Live your truth. There's always someone to relate to, even if you can't find someone in person. Just keep believing and find them. My friend group is all very accepting and very accommodating. We joke that all the gays flock to each other because we all found each other."

ADARA (18)

"I currently work at a company that's super accepting and everyone uses my pronouns. And if people don't know my pronouns, they always correct them when they figure it out. It's amazing."

QUEER BOOKS AND MEDIA THAT CELEBRATE ACCEPTANCE

BUT I'M A CHEERLEADER . . . . . Romantic Comedy Movie
Directed by Jamie Babbit

THE OWL HOUSE . . . . Animated TV Show
Created by Dana Terrace

THE HOUSE IN THE CERULEAN SEA . . . YA Fantasy Novel
Written by TJ Klune

LOVE, SIMON . . . . Romantic Comedy Movie
Directed by Greg Berlanti

MODERN FAMILY . . . . Comedy TV Show
Created by Steven levitan
& Christopher LLoyd

WHAT IF IT'S US . . . . YA Romance Novel
Written by Becky Albertalli
& Adam Silvera

STEVEN UNIVERSE . . . . Animated TV Show
Created by Rebecca Sugar

FELIX EVER AFTER . . . . YA Novel
Written by Kacen Callendar

KNOW OF A GREAT SHOW, BOOK, OR MOVIE? SHARE IT WITH #SHAREQUEERCHEER

THE POWER OF SELF-ACCEPTANCE

Self-acceptance has been shown to increase happiness and self-worth, grant autonomy, and even give you a sense of freedom! Don't wait for someone else to accept you—be your own champion! Embrace and celebrate every part of yourself, fabs and flubs, because your sexuality, gender, values, dreams, and talents matter!

WAYS TO INCREASE YOUR SELF-ACCEPTANCE

- ○ List your abilities and strengths.
- ○ Ignore your inner critic.
- ○ Connect with people who appreciate you.
- ○ List five reasons to be proud of your identity.
- ○ Practice self-compassion and forgive yourself!

AM I ALLOWED TO TELL SOMEONE THEY ARE BEING HATEFUL, HOMOPHOBIC, OR TRANSPHOBIC?

MAKE SURE YOU ARE SAFE AND DO SO IN A WAY THAT MANAGES YOUR EXPECTATIONS.

1 A DAY IN OUR LIFE

Take your friends or family members on a queer day outing that showcases the queer community. Eat at a queer-owned restaurant or attend a pride family picnic. Show them your local LGBTQ+ center, queer-owned comic store, etc. Go to a queer museum or art exhibit. Attend a performance by the Gay Men's Chorus or watch a queer-themed play. You could also do crafts or projects together, like making rainbow friendship bracelets. Be creative and think outside of the box.

2 MOVIE MAGIC

Have a queer movie night with friends or family you'd like to "get you" just a little bit more, especially if it's hard for you to explain. Ask if they would be willing to watch a film that has characters or themes that show aspects of your queer identity. You could offer a Q&A after the film or just leave it at "the main character is me." Don't forget the rainbow popcorn!

3 BRACELET BUDDIES

Make a bracelet with a positive phrase such as "I accept you." Pick a friend to give it to and give them a genuine compliment. Invent a rule for passing the bracelet to another friend within your group. Try to pick something rare, for example, when someone has a rough day, achieves a goal, wears orange, etc. Don't forget to compliment the receiver every time it's passed. Soon, it'll come back to you!

STRONGER TOGETHER

CARE TO SHARE?

#ShareQueerCheer

RAINBOW AFFIRMATIONS

I decide what I believe about myself. My self-worth is not determined by the opinions of others.

My sexual orientation and gender identity deserve awareness and respect.

I will not minimize myself to protect the feelings of others.

I am allowed to distance myself from willfully ignorant friends, relatives, or spiritual leaders.

It's not the job of others to like me. It's mine.

I have the power to decide whether to accept or reject how I am treated.

WHAT MAKES A FAMILY?

There is no one-size-fits-all definition of family. Families come in all sorts of shapes and sizes, and they're formed through a variety of ways, such as birth, adoption, marriage, or friendship. Families can be made up of all sorts of people, like single parents, foster parents, two moms or two dads, siblings, relatives, and even fur babies! The vital part of a family is that they love and support you no matter what. Sometimes, the families we're born into are not how we wish them to be. They don't support us, or they are lost to us. It's okay to be sad about that, but it doesn't mean you have to be without a family. You can seek out family members who uplift and support you or even create your own chosen family! Our community is known for found family! We find people to fill the roles missing in our lives. You can have multiple families, too! So go ahead, define who YOUR family is, then make it special with meaningful traditions and memories together.

"A HOME ISN'T ALWAYS THE HOUSE WE LIVE IN. IT'S ALSO THE PEOPLE WE CHOOSE TO SURROUND OURSELVES WITH." —TJ KLUNE

Conversations On FAMILY

PARKER (16)

"I grew up in a household that was just my dad, my brother, and me. My mom lived in a different house because they were divorced. One of the main things that me and my dad both realized is I never had a mother figure that was actually there for me. It was always my dad."

EVAN (18)

"When my boyfriend and I started dating, his parents were a lot more accepting than mine, and they kind of adopted me into their family. At the time, all I felt I had for family were his parents, but my mom and dad have since come around and they absolutely adore my boyfriend."

LIS (17)

"For me, family has never been who you are born into. It's whoever will support you and love you unconditionally. For me, I've had a hard time because I've never had a real father figure in my life, so I've adapted to my father figure being other people's dads because they support me and they're there for me if I need anything."

CHACE (17)

"From my experience with family, there are two types of it. One is biological and the second is found. And both of those families can be equally as important, or as unimportant, as any individual person wants them to be."

NACEY (19)

"Family is important, but so is a healthy living environment. I can value my family without having to be at their beck and call 24/7. Family for me is someone who shows unconditional love and allows you to express yourself without any judgment. If they don't respect your boundaries, they aren't real family."

JACKSON (18)

"Find other supportive people in your life. That's important for everyone. If your family isn't supportive, find people who are."

TRADITIONS FOR YOUR FAMILY OR FOUND FAMILY

Check out some of these family traditions. Maybe you'd like to do one of these with your family, or maybe you can come up with one of your own!

- WATCH THE SUNSET/SUNRISE ON SPECIAL DAYS
- HAVE A SCRAPBOOK ASSEMBLY PARTY
- TAKE A YEARLY PHOTO IN MATCHING PJS
- TAKE AN ANNUAL THEME PARK TRIP
- HIKE TO A SPECIAL PLACE
- WATCH THE PRIDE PARADE, OR MAYBE EVEN BE IN IT
- HOLD A REGULAR BOARD GAME NIGHT
- HONOR AN ANCESTOR
- CARVE PUMPKINS
- HAVE AN UGLY SWEATER PARTY
- HOLD A SUMMER BBQ
- BAKE A SPECIAL RECIPE TOGETHER ON A HOLIDAY
- LIGHT A LANTERN ON A SPECIAL DAY
- GO APPLE PICKING EVERY FALL
- GO STAR-GAZING DURING A METEOR SHOWER
- ENJOY HOT COCOA AND S'MORES ON THE FIRST DAY OF WINTER

STORIES ABOUT FOUND FAMILY

MOVIES

RENT
(2005) PG-13

GUARDIANS OF THE GALAXY
(2014) PG-13

NIMONA
(2023) PG

BOOKS

SIX OF CROWS
by Leigh Bardugo (2016) Ages 14–17

THE WITCH KING
by H. E. Edgmon (2021) Ages 13–17

AS FAR AS YOU'LL TAKE ME
by Phil Stamper (2022) Ages 13–17

TV SHOWS

GHOSTS
(2021) TV-PG

STRANGER THINGS
(2016) TV-14

AVATAR: THE LAST AIRBENDER
(2005–2008) TV-Y7-FV

1 A SEAT AT THE TABLE

Plan a holiday dinner for queer friends or community members who don't have accepting families. Perhaps your family is even willing to have them over! Consider adding some fun queer elements to the dinner, like rainbow mashed potatoes for Thanksgiving or heart-shaped cookies with Pride flags for Valentine's Day. Make it fun and accepting for everyone.

2 FAMILY SUPPORT

Research the queer family resources available on the PFLAG website and find information that might be helpful for your family. Look up your local PFLAG chapter, find an event, and invite your family to attend with you.

3 ROYAL REPRESENTATION

Create a family symbol, motto, or crest to represent the unity of your family. When it's finished, decide how you will use it. You could frame it and display it in your house, put it on a T-shirt and have everyone wear it during a family outing (maybe even Pride), put it on your mailbox, use it on holiday cards, etc. Be creative!

STRONGER TOGETHER

QUEER QUESTIONS

WHAT IS SOMETHING YOU CAN DO TO IMPROVE A RELATIONSHIP WITH SOMEONE IN YOUR FAMILY?

ASK YOURSELF

QUEER QUESTIONS

HOW IS YOUR FAMILY DIFFERENT FROM OR SIMILAR TO OTHER FAMILIES?

ASK YOURSELF

QUEER QUESTIONS

WHAT'S ONE THING A FAMILY MEMBER COULD DO TO HELP YOU FEEL MORE SUPPORTED? ARE YOU COMFORTABLE ASKING FOR THIS?

ASK YOURSELF

CARE TO SHARE?

#ShareQueerCheer

RAINBOW AFFIRMATIONS

I deserve a family who loves and supports me unconditionally.

I am allowed to expect my family to treat me with dignity.

I get to choose what family means to me.

I can create a family and community of my choice.

I am not required to educate or endure relatives who refuse to acknowledge my truth.

I am irreplaceable to those who love me.

QUALITY FRIENDSHIPS

There are many levels of friendship, from the acquaintance you paired up with in science class to your ride-or-die besties who know your embarrassing secrets and wear matching Swiftie shirts with you to Pride. These bonds enrich our lives, providing joy and relief from stress. **Strong bonds take time and care to build,** and they start with choosing who you let in. Do you want to keep a friendship casual or develop a deeper connection? Either way, **invest your time in friends who accept you and support your dreams.** True friends bring joy and add that extra sparkle to your life. If someone bails after you come out to them, they were never a real friend to begin with. And who needs that? Not you. You deserve so much more!

YOU DESERVE IT!

YOU DESERVE FRIENDS WHO ACCEPT YOU AS YOU ARE.

YOU DESERVE FRIENDS WHO ACCEPT YOUR ORIENTATION AND IDENTITIES.

YOU DESERVE FRIENDS WHO MAKE YOU FEEL GOOD ABOUT YOURSELF.

WHY? BECAUSE YOU'RE WORTH IT!

Conversations On FRIENDSHIP

CHACE (17)

"I try to find people with the same sense of humor as me because humor is kind of a centric communicator and I'm somebody who likes to make a lot of jokes. I'm at my best when I feel like I can joke with the people I'm around. That's a really positive thing for me."

ADARA (18)

"When I was younger, I wrote fanfiction and someone really loved my stories. They gave me a code to their Discord, and we became friends through that. All my other queer friends, I met through school in drama practice."

JACKSON (18)

"I met my best friend in first grade. They're nonbinary. We really just get each other. A lot of that is because we've known each other so long, but the fact that we're both autistic definitely plays a role in that, too. Whenever I need a friend, they're always there for me, and I try to do the same for them."

CONSTANCE (19)

"Everyone is capable of being worthy of having good friends, and they will find you when it's the right time."

NACEY (19)

"My best friend is not just a good friend, she's a good human. She's obviously not perfect and there are times we argue. The times we argue I look back on the way she encourages me to handle it. She makes me want to be a better human being."

EVAN (18)

"In friendships I value someone who is accepting. Someone who is genuine."

IT'S IMPORTANT TO REFLECT ON WHAT QUALITIES WE LOOK FOR IN A GOOD FRIEND. ASK YOURSELF WHAT YOU LOOK FOR IN A FRIEND.

Is it:

- How smart they are?
- What kind of home they live in?
- What faith they follow?
- What size they are?
- How honest they are?
- If they like the same movies, TV shows, or food as you?
- How much you can trust them?
- What kind of car their parents drive?
- How much fun you have with them?
- What morals and values they hold?
- How popular they are?
- The brand of clothes they wear or how they style their hair?
- How much they gossip about other people?
- How much they listen when you share your problems?
- How dependable they are?

GOOD FRIEND HABITS

Be present with each other

Actively listen when someone is talking

Make each other laugh

Be there for one another

Check in with each other

Remember little things to show you pay attention

Celebrate milestones together

Spend quality time together

Ask how you can help each other

Address each other's needs

Lift each other up

Try These ACTIVITIES

1 BLINDFOLDED COOKING

This activity will test your trust. Get together with a friend and plan a basic meal that doesn't involve knives or cooking. Think sandwich or no-bake energy bites. Put all the ingredients on the counter. One of you puts a blindfold on and makes the food while the other talks them through the steps. To ensure that no one purposely messes things up, both of you have to eat it when it's done.

2 SPILL THE TEA

It's tea time, darlings! Gather round the table with some friends and a question deck that dives into some deep friendship topics. Take turns pulling a card and asking each other questions. Be honest with each other!

3 SECRET LANGUAGE

Create a secret language with your besties. Write down each letter of the alphabet. Assign each letter a unique symbol to represent it. Then write each other secret messages using your new symbols. If decoding isn't your thing, try creating a secret handshake.

SELF QUEERY
QUEER QUESTIONS
WHAT VALUES ARE IMPORTANT TO HAVE IN A FRIEND?
ASK YOURSELF
QUEER QUESTIONS
HOW WELL DO YOU THINK MOST PEOPLE KNOW YOU? DO YOU FEEL COMFORTABLE SHARING PERSONAL THOUGHTS, OPINIONS, AND MEMORIES?
ASK YOURSELF
QUEER QUESTIONS
HOW SUPPORTED DO YOU FEEL BY THE PEOPLE IN YOUR LIFE? HOW DO YOU PROVIDE SUPPORT IN RETURN?
ASK YOURSELF
QUEER QUESTIONS
DO YOU HAVE FRIENDS WHO ARE DIFFERENT RACES OR RELIGIONS THAN YOU? DOES THAT EVER AFFECT HOW YOU RELATE TO EACH OTHER?
ASK YOURSELF
CARE TO SHARE?
#ShareQueerCheer

RAINBOW AFFIRMATIONS

I deserve quality friendships.

I deserve friends who will love and support me when I'm making difficult decisions.

I do not need to be "healed" to be deserving of love and friendship.

I deserve allies in my life who make me feel safe and supported in all spaces.

I deserve friends who never ask me to apologize for being who I am.

I can take all the time I need before I let people in.

LOVE, ROMANCE & INTIMACY

Exploring deeper physical, romantic, emotional, or sexual connections can electrify your world and bring incredible emotions like love, hope, excitement, and happiness. We may even get butterflies when asking someone out on a first date or feel proud when we reach anniversaries and milestones together. Many partner dynamics and their roles can come with different expectations, values, and agreements, so you may need to consider and experiment to define what is right for you. **Regardless of your relationship type, remember that you deserve to be treated with respect.** Communicating with your partners and paying attention to each other's boundaries is essential, especially if you're getting intimate. **Take time to work out with your partners what you both enjoy and feel comfortable with.** Don't be afraid to try new things, as long as you're being safe and having fun!

"THE POWER OF LOVE IS THAT IT SEES ALL PEOPLE."
—DASHANNE STOKES

Conversations On

LOVE, ROMANCE, & INTIMACY

CONSTANCE (19)

"Trans people have a tendency to get into abusive relationships because a lot of the time we feel like we need to settle when it comes to intimacy. I'd like to remind any trans person out there that you are deserving of the love you want. You expect your friends and loved ones to fully accept you being trans, so why should that change when it's romantic love?"

JACKSON (18)

"Setting clear boundaries and expectations in the beginning could possibly prevent you from being put in a difficult situation. And if you find yourself uncomfortable with something in the moment, and you feel like you should say something, then you should definitely do that. It's better to communicate something uncomfortable than to let something that you're not comfortable with happen."

CALLAHAN (18)

"I'm very upfront about being trans for my safety. And everyone I've dated has been my friend first, so they've all known I was trans before dating me. My girlfriend and I are just starting to introduce intimacy. I don't know what is going to trigger my dysphoria. There are things that sound like they would be cool and okay, but in practice, they might not be, so it's important to be upfront about boundaries."

ALIA (17)

"It's a good idea to get in a relationship with someone you're already friends with because you already know the person, feel safe with them, and know their sexuality. Rushing into things with someone you don't know isn't always safe."

EVAN (18)

"We cuddled in the beginning of our relationship, but we didn't kiss until our first anniversary. Anything more than that, we didn't do until after two and a half years. We were always sure to communicate our comfort before we moved forward with anything new."

PERCY (18)

"In my experience, there's a lot of pressure to date someone and prove you're queer, but it is really important for me to remember that I don't need to be in a relationship to be queer."

PARKER (16)

"I'm not someone who thinks they constantly have to be in a relationship. I don't want a relationship that is very serious or can impact the things that I want to do, because, at some point in my life, I want to go to London and take culinary classes. I never want a relationship to get in the way of that."

REMEMBER...

- Consent can change mid-activity and should be honored if changed.
- Romance does not always lead to intimacy. Asexual people exist.
- Intimacy does not always involve romance. Aromantic people exist.
- You define your romantic and sexual relationships how you want.
- Don't feel pressured to prove your sexual identity or gender to anyone.
- Your partners and activity do not always determine your orientation. For example, if someone bisexual is in a same-sex relationship, that does not make them gay.
- If you choose to be sexually intimate, be safe. Know your HIV/STD status and use protection.
- Consider speaking to a healthcare professional about using PrEP (medicine that can reduce your chances of getting HIV when taken as prescribed) and/or birth control.

QUEER LOVE IS...

VALID

NORMAL

BEAUTIFUL

INSPIRING

GREAT

IMPORTANT

MAGNIFICENT

GLORIOUS

SAFE ONLINE DATING TIPS

- Don't trust a photo; do a reverse image search.
- Meet in a public place.
- Tell a friend you trust where you're going, including the address.

1 TABLE TENNIS TALK

Take a moment to share each other's boundaries and comfort levels. To do this, sit across from each other at a table and take turns asking questions about boundaries, such as "Are you comfortable with kissing in public?" Count to three, then at the same time, hold up a sign or a ping-pong paddle that you have labeled with either "YES," "NO" or "MAYBE." This way you can answer honestly without being influenced by each other. If someone answers "MAYBE," talk about it to get a better understanding of their thoughts.

2 REMEMBER ME

Test your knowledge of each other. Grab a pen or pencil and a piece of paper, and take turns asking questions about each other. For example, what is your favorite movie? What would I buy first if I won a million dollars? And does the toilet paper go over or under the roll? Write down your guesses for each question. When you're done, reveal your answers and discuss!

3 SURPRISE DATE NIGHT

Check your partner's availability, and then plan a surprise date. Don't tell them what the actual activity will be, but make sure it's something fun they will enjoy. Maybe a picnic at the park, a hike, a pottery class, or even bowling. Consider making this a monthly tradition and alternate who does the planning. If you pick activities you haven't done before, you'll grow through fun new experiences together!

STRONGER TOGETHER

SELF QUEERY
QUEER QUESTIONS
WHAT ARE YOUR EXPECTATIONS IN A RELATIONSHIP?
ASK YOURSELF
QUEER QUESTIONS
HOW IMPORTANT DO YOU THINK IT IS TO ESTABLISH A FRIENDSHIP PRIOR TO DATING SOMEONE? WHY?
ASK YOURSELF
QUEER QUESTIONS
WHAT ARE YOUR BOUNDARIES, BOTH PHYSICAL AND EMOTIONAL? WHAT'S A RELATIONSHIP DEAL-BREAKER FOR YOU?
ASK YOURSELF
QUEER QUESTIONS
WHAT DO YOU THINK ABOUT MARRIAGE OR HAVING KIDS? ARE THOSE THINGS IMPORTANT TO YOU?
ASK YOURSELF
CARE TO SHARE?
#ShareQueerCheer

RAINBOW AFFIRMATIONS

I am worthy of love, and I deserve a healthy relationship.

I have the right to say yes/no/maybe, or change my mind.

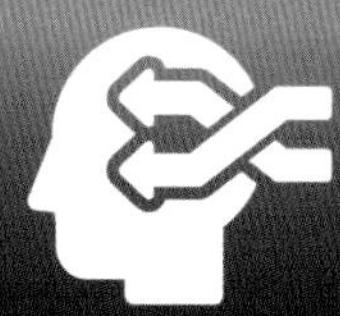

My partners and I decide what our relationships look like, regardless of outside expectations and stereotypes.

I can move forward at my own pace, and I don't have to rush into anything I'm not ready for.

Being single does not diminish my worth.

I give and receive unconditional love.

THE CATAGORY IS...

SCHOOL

Whether you go to public, private, or home school, and whether you attend online or in person, one thing is for certain. You spend a great deal of your time there! That's why it's important to ensure your environment is an inclusive safe space where you can learn all the important skills you need free of harassment and discrimination. If you're constantly hiding who you are, you can't give 100 percent of your focus to your studies. Everyone learns better when they can be their true, authentic selves. That's when you can truly shine!

EDUCATIONAL ENVIRONMENT

How many hours, days, and years have you clocked at school? A LOT! It's a major part of your life, and you deserve to be comfortable as your authentic self while you're there. Hopefully, your school is all about diversity and inclusion, because **you deserve nothing less than support and respect from your teachers and classmates.** But if your school is non-affirming and maybe even has policies that prevent the expression of your sexual orientation or gender identity, you may need to find some safer spaces. Don't be afraid to tell a supportive teacher, family member, or friend who can help you navigate your way through school. They may even help find a place where you have a sense of belonging.

MANY TEENS HAVE FOUND OTHER QUEER PALS IN CLASSES LIKE BAND, THEATER, OR CHOIR. DO YOU HAVE AN INTEREST IN TRYING ONE OF THOSE CLASSES?

QUEER FACTS!

THE THIRD THURSDAY IN OCTOBER IS SPIRIT DAY! ON THIS DAY, PEOPLE WEAR PURPLE TO SUPPORT QUEER YOUTH AND GIVE A VISIBLE SIGN AGAINST BULLYING.

Conversations On EDUCATIONAL ENVIRONMENTS

ALIA (17)

"At my school, we have a system set up where I can enter my name and pronouns and where they can use them (for example, announcements, parents, yearbook) so students can use them at school but don't necessarily have to use them with parents. That's very important. That's obviously not possible in all states—it's great having the option of finding that safe space."

ADARA (18)

"The policies at my high school were kind of anti-gay. For example, if you were assigned male at birth (AMAB), you weren't allowed to wear dresses to dances. There was one girl who was AMAB, and she wore a suit so she wouldn't be stopped from coming into the dance, but she brought a dress to change into after. When she was switching into her dress, a teacher came by and told her she wasn't allowed to do that, but they would let her as it got closer to the end of the night. So, the teachers were super accepting even though the school rules were not."

ZIE (17)

"One of my teachers was queer and she was who I would go to for any sort of problems when it came to being queer. She was my supporter. And band is a safe place for us at school. I have a lot of queer friends in band, and we joke, if you're having trouble with being yourself or finding other queer people, join band."

ELIXIR (16)

"Teachers are accommodating at my school. They call me by my name as long as I tell them at the beginning of the year. My friends are cool, too, but other people, not so much. I'm still called by my deadname, even by people who never knew me before. Some people went out of their way to find my deadname as a way to mock me. I don't care what bigoted people think of me, though. I'm going to live my life and have fun. I don't tolerate people being mean to me. I stopped hanging out with people who continued to deadname me and it helped."

PARKER (16)

"By the time I switched to an alternative school, I had my name and everything long enough that it wasn't an issue. Overall, the alternative school is pretty inclusive. They're really supportive of the students and give me a lot more one-on-one time to help me progress through classes, which helps a lot with my disability and everything. I think a different school would have been more difficult."

PERCY (18)

"My high school had a few gender-neutral bathrooms, and for new classes, we always introduced ourselves by saying our names and pronouns and that was great. I was able to identify other people that way. We didn't have queer rep in our textbooks or videos, but there were queer books in the library which was awesome. And our librarians were super great. They had a display for queer books that had been banned."

SIGNS OF AN INCLUSIVE SCHOOL

Respects all identities and adopts policies to protect them

Anti-discrimination policy includes LGBTQ+ students

Inclusive language on forms and communications

Opportunities to find support from peers and staff

Confidentiality and privacy in school records

Inclusive posters and signage on campus

Teachers educated in equal and supportive treatment

Diverse/LGBTQ+ faculty and staff hired

Inclusive dress codes that allow you to be you

Inclusive sports teams and clubs

All types of families welcomed

Designated staff for challenges, experiences, or questions

Policies to reduce and prevent bullying

Opportunities to share experiences and perspectives

Inclusive and comprehensive curriculum/textbooks

Inclusive spaces such as an LGBTQ+ center and GSA

Gender-neutral bathrooms/changing rooms

Queer-inclusive books in the library

Resources, compassion, and care year-round
(not just June!)

THIS IS A SAFE SPACE

PROUD to be ME!

EMBRACE WHO YOU ARE

EXPRESS YOURSELF

ARE PUBLIC SCHOOLS REQUIRED TO ALLOW STUDENTS TO ESTABLISH A GSA?

According to the Equal Access Act (which can be found on the United States Department of Education's website), if your school has at least one student-led group or club, then YES!

There are many laws that impact queer youth on local, state, and federal levels. Check out organizations such as Lambda Legal, GLAD, the National Center for Lesbian Rights, and the ACLU to stay informed on current laws and to get help if your rights are violated.

1 GET INFORMED

Take some time to educate yourself on the workings of your school. Research their policies and procedures on inclusivity and diversity. Are there any that concern you? Pay close attention to sections on discrimination, bullying, dress codes, athletics, bathroom access, school dances, student records and privacy, gender transitions, and names and pronouns.

2 ATTEND A MEETING

Research your local school board. Who are the board members and what are their stances? What agenda items do they have for their upcoming meetings? Attend a meeting to see how they work.

3 SEE THE SIGNS

Search your school for queer-inclusive signs/posters and keep track of how many you can find. Look for rainbows, gender-neutral bathroom signs, and phrases like "Everyone is Welcome Here." If you can't find any, ask a school official if you can put some up, if you feel safe and comfortable doing so.

STRONGER TOGETHER

SELF QUEERY
QUEER QUESTIONS
WHICH TEACHER DO YOU FEEL MOST COMFORTABLE TALKING TO? WHY?
ASK YOURSELF
QUEER QUESTIONS
IN WHAT WAYS DO YOU FEEL COMFORTABLE EXPRESSING YOUR QUEER IDENTITIES AT SCHOOL? IN WHAT WAYS DO YOU HOLD BACK?
ASK YOURSELF
QUEER QUESTIONS
DO YOU FEEL CONFIDENT ENOUGH IN YOUR KNOWLEDGE OF SCHOOL POLICIES AND PROCEDURES TO BE AN ADVOCATE FOR YOURSELF AND FELLOW STUDENTS?
ASK YOURSELF
QUEER QUESTIONS
WOULD YOU FEEL COMFORTABLE GOING TO A SCHOOL DANCE IN YOUR PREFERRED CLOTHING OR WITH A DATE OF THE SAME GENDER?
ASK YOURSELF
CARE TO SHARE?
#ShareQueerCheer

RAINBOW AFFIRMATIONS

I deserve respect from my classmates, teachers, and school officials.

I belong just as much as everyone else.

I am a positive contributor to my school.

I can succeed in spite of my surroundings.

I have the power to seek out safe spaces at school.

I am committed to taking advantage of available resources and making the most of my educational journey.

PROMOTING INCLUSION

When schools are inclusive and supportive of queer students, self-esteem for everyone in the school is likely to increase! And the good news is that, even if your school is not where you want it to be, there are things you can do to try to improve it. Plenty of **teens across the US have changed their school environment for the better** by doing things like starting GSAs, implementing gender-neutral bathrooms, starting queer education workshops, and even helping elect queer-friendly school boards! Here are instances where teens made changes at their school. After reading them, think about ways that you and your friends can make your school more inclusive.

The 2021 Adolescent Behaviors and Experiences Survey conducted by the CDC found that, when schools implement LGBTQ+-supportive policies and procedures, ALL students benefit, not just queer students! Schools reported having a decrease in emotional distress, reduced violence and harassment, and an increase in mental health.

CITE: WWW.CDC.GOV/HEALTHYYOUTH/SAFE-SUPPORTIVE-ENVIRONMENTS/LGBTQ-POLICIES-PRACTICES.HTM

Conversations On
PROMOTING INCLUSION

ADARA (18)

"I wrote an email to my school asking if I could wear a suit to graduation, and I was totally prepared to not go to the ceremony, but surprisingly they said I could go dressed in a suit! I liked being able to fit in with the more masculine people and it was definitely nice not having to wear a dress."

CALLAHAN (18)

"My school choir director was very traditional about what we had to wear, but I talked to her and I was like, 'Hey I don't want to wear a dress. Can I wear a suit instead?' and she said I could! Quite a few choir kids came up to me after the performance and said they were going to ask the director if they could wear a suit. That was really cool because just me being who I am inspired other people to find a way to be comfortable with themselves, too."

LUCY (19)

"A bunch of us who didn't have a prom, or had an issue going for like some reason or another, got together and threw our own. We got to wear what we wanted, think up color schemes, and even made invites on Canva. It was really fun."

JACKSON (18)

"One of my friends had two moms and they talked to them about wanting a gender-neutral bathroom in our school. The four of us worked to find supportive teachers to back us up until the head of the school agreed to allow us to send a survey to all the teachers asking if they would support it. We eventually got a gender-neutral bathroom installed in our school because we kept pushing for it and we didn't give up."

LIS (17)

"I do the Day of Silence every year and pass out note cards to people that want them. One kid was talking about how their parents didn't support them and I kind of helped them get through that and find people they can be around. So, just by being out and open, you could be showing someone else who's struggling that they're not alone."

ALIA (17)

"My friend and I started a GSA club because we were having a lot of bad hallway experiences. I wrote an essay about why we needed it and we brought it to the principal, and we were able to create our GSA club because of that. Having a space to talk openly about our experiences in a safe judgment-free zone was really helpful."

Volume 6, Issue 17

Queer Cheer

STUDENT NEWS

STUDENTS PROTECTING EDUCATION: THE POWER OF YOUTH ACTIVISM!

When sophomores Jill and Luke learned people were trying to ban books from their school library, they gathered friends from the Racial Equity Alliance Club and attended the next board meeting to speak out. "You could see from their list that they had an agenda," explained Luke. "Every single book they were trying to get rid of had to do with either race, sexuality, gender identity, or sexism. It was really upsetting." Teachers, parents, and other community members joined to speak out, and in the end, they won!

After successfully fighting against the book ban, Jill and Luke founded Students Protecting Education to promote diversity and inclusion. They soon discovered there was more work to do. When they learned that the book banners were running for the local school board elections, they jumped back into action. Jill and Luke identified and supported three candidates running on a pro-student platform.

Despite not being old enough to vote, the members of Students Protecting Education made a difference by phone banking, posting on social media, and appearing on the news.

FIGHT 4 UR RIGHTS!

Their efforts paid off because all three candidates they supported won the election.

"It's unusual for people our age to speak up, at least in our area," said Jill. "So, for the board to see students, and say, 'They actually care about this, maybe we should listen for once,' I think was very eye-opening."

Students Protecting Education also campaigned for a proposition allowing a student to serve on the school board. That proposition passed by a three-to-one margin!

Jill and Luke have had a lot of success. Students Protecting Education now has student members in twenty-two states! These teens prove that youth activism can be a powerful force for change and that young people can make a difference in the world.

www.studentsproed.org

ACTION ITEMS!

Ideas to help bring more inclusivity to your school environment.

BE CREATIVE—Find fun ways to inject inclusivity where you can! This can be school projects, notebook doodles, Pink Proms, or poetry clubs.

INCREASE ACCESS—Ask your librarian if they can stock queer books if they don't already, or suggest additional titles to increase their current inventory.

ORGANIZE A ROUNDTABLE—Invite teachers and students to come and listen to ideas for promoting inclusivity.

INFORM OTHERS—Organize a media campaign or education talk showcasing the benefits of inclusivity for all students.

OFFER RESOURCES—Provide resources like inclusive ready-to-use lesson plans, educational books, and organizations that help promote inclusion.

ASK FOR TRAINING—Check to see if your school provides inclusivity and sensitivity training for faculty. If they don't, ask them to start.

KNOW YOUR RIGHTS—Research school policies and education laws on your local, state, and federal levels.

REPORT HARASSMENT—If your school is not addressing harassment or bullying, consider reporting it to the superintendent, school board, outside lawyers, or the ACLU.

FIND SUPPORT—Look for resources and allies who will help promote change and support your mental health.

CONSIDER ALTERNATIVES—It's okay to research a more supportive classroom, teacher, or school environment.

GLSEN and the GSA Network are both wonderful organizations that help promote inclusivity in schools. Check out their websites for more ideas or for support!

GLSEN: www.glsen.org
GSA Network: www.gsanetwork.org

Try These ACTIVITIES

1 SEARCH FOR INSPIRATION

Teens all around the country, and even the world, are stepping up to make positive changes at their schools. Search the web to find more inspiring stories and share them using #ShareQueerCheer to inspire others.

2 HOST A SPEAKER

Get permission to invite a leader in the queer community to speak for Pride Month or LGBTQ+ History Month.

3 SPREAD THE WORD

Write an article for your school newspaper or newsletter about an important piece of queer history for LGBTQ+ History Month.

STRONGER TOGETHER

QUEER QUESTIONS

IN WHAT WAYS MIGHT YOU MAKE YOUR SCHOOL MORE INCLUSIVE?

ASK YOURSELF

QUEER QUESTIONS

WOULD A DIFFERENT SCHOOL OR AN ONLINE/HOME SCHOOL BE BETTER FOR YOUR EDUCATION AND MENTAL HEALTH?

ASK YOURSELF

QUEER QUESTIONS

WHAT WOULD A MORE INCLUSIVE SCHOOL ENVIRONMENT LOOK LIKE?

ASK YOURSELF

QUEER QUESTIONS

WHICH SCHOOL OR COMMUNITY ALLIES (EDUCATORS, GUARDIANS, POLITICIANS, ETC.) COULD HELP MAKE YOUR SCHOOL MORE INCLUSIVE?

ASK YOURSELF

CARE TO SHARE?

#ShareQueerCheer

RAINBOW AFFIRMATIONS

I can find opportunities to celebrate equality, inclusion, and diversity in my school.

I have a positive impact on the school community.

I am an advocate for myself and my peers and am allowed to voice my concerns to authority figures.

My concerns about my school are valid.

I am empowered to create or seek the learning environment I need.

I am grateful for the teachers and school staff who support me.

FILLING IN EDUCATION GAPS

Did you know that a gay man, Bayard Rustin, organized the 1963 march where Martin Luther King Jr. gave his famous "I Have A Dream" speech? Or that the first American woman in space, Sally Ride, was in a committed same-sex relationship for twenty-seven years? Or that a trans man, Alan Hart, pioneered the use of X-rays to screen for tuberculosis? How cool is that? **People in the queer community have done amazing things throughout history**, but unfortunately, it's rare that anyone ever learns about LGBTQ+ contributions in school. Many students don't get comprehensive sex education, either. **We encourage you to be your own advocate in filling in these education gaps**. Reach out to your local LGBTQ+ center, search credible online sources, and read queer history books. And don't be afraid to ask your local librarian for resources and help. They're typically great advocates and allies for free information! Trust us, a well-rounded education will support you in a variety of ways!

OCTOBER IS LGBTQ+ HISTORY MONTH IN THE US!

October was chosen by Missouri teacher Rodney Wilson to coincide with National Coming Out Day (October 11) and the anniversary of the first two marches on Washington (1979 and 1987) for LGBTQ rights.

Conversations On EDUCATION GAPS

CADENCE (13)

"I feel like our school is inclusive because they have a GSA, they fly the Pride flag during Pride month, and they talk about orientation and identity in sex-ed. But even with all that, we never learn about queer people in history."

ALIA (17)

"In my area we have a lot of different organizations that do programming for youth, but I think a lot of it is also online and it's about finding the right places. If you're not able to get resources because of your family, you can do deep dives on Wikipedia or watch great documentaries about queer things on Netflix."

LIS (17)

"Most of what I learned about the queer community came from social media or I learned about them in GSA. I've learned about different parades and the reason we have pride month, and why GLSEN celebrates the Day of Silence. We should learn these things in school instead of having to search on the internet."

NACEY (19)

"When the AIDS pandemic was talked about, it was wiped through like 'this happened' with no info on how or why it happened. I did more research on my own and anytime something happens in the community, it sparks my interest in the history and I try to educate myself."

ADARA (18)

"We had sex-ed in seventh grade, but that was definitely not queer focused at all. I learned about that by reading online, typically through fanfiction and Tumblr."

CHACE (17)

"I love the library at my school. I think we might have even had like a full section on queer authors. I remember for Pride month, some of the younger kids were being read to. I was in the library at the same time and the library teacher was like, 'This was written by a gay man!' "

TOPICS THAT NEED MORE ATTENTION

HOW CAN YOU FILL IN THESE EDUCATION GAPS?

- THE HISTORY OF PRIDE
- QUEER HEROES AND ICONS
- QUEER HISTORY
- QUEER CULTURE AND SYMBOLISM
- GENDER IDENTITY AND SEXUAL ORIENTATION
- LGBTQ+ RIGHTS AND LAWS
- LGBTQ+ ISSUES
- THE HISTORY OF RACISM, ANTISEMITISM, AND SEXISM
- IMPACT OF DISCRIMINATION, INEQUALITY, AND INTERSECTIONALITY
- HOW TO DEFEND AGAINST INEQUALITY AND DISCRIMINATION
- CLIMATE CHANGE
- SELF-DEFENSE AND SURVIVAL
- HOW CREDIT CARDS, CHECKING, SAVINGS, AND LOANS WORK
- CREDIT CARD USE AND COMPOUNDING INTEREST
- HOW TO FILE TAXES
- BUDGETING, RETIREMENT, AND INVESTMENTS
- INTERVIEW, RESUME, AND APPLICATION SKILLS
- NETWORKING SKILLS
- CAR/HOME BUYING, MAINTENANCE, AND REPAIR
- COMPREHENSIVE AND INCLUSIVE SEX-ED
- RENTING AN APARTMENT AND TENANT RIGHTS
- HOW HEALTH, LIFE, HOUSE, AND CAR INSURANCE WORKS
- EMPLOYMENT LAWS AND RIGHTS
- VOTING RIGHTS AND HOW TO VOTE
- PARENTING SKILLS
- HOW TO COOK
- BASIC FIRST AID

SOURCES TO LEARN FROM

- LIBRARIES
- LGBTQ+ CENTERS
- YOUTUBE
- TEACHERS
- REPUTABLE WEBSITES & PODCASTS
- FAMILY OR FRIENDS

There's lots of misinformation out there. Make sure you're using a discerning eye and finding information from sources that are honest and have done their research.

LGBTQ+ MEDIA TO LEARN ABOUT QUEER HISTORY

Books

THE IMITATION GAME: ALAN TURING DECODED
by Jim Ottaviani
A graphic novel biography about Alan Turing, a gay mathematician and scientist who helped decipher German encrypted correspondence and saved numerous lives during World War II.

QUEER, THERE, AND EVERYWHERE: SECOND EDITION: 27 PEOPLE WHO CHANGED THE WORLD
by Sarah Prager
Profiles of twenty-seven queer people from different cultures and explains their impact on world history.

OCTOBER MOURNING: A SONG FOR MATTHEW SHEPARD
by Lesléa Newman
A collection of sixty-eight poems that chronicle the final moments of Matthew Shepard, a young gay man, who was killed in one of the most notorious hate crimes in recent US history.

Documentaries

EDIE & THEA: A VERY LONG ENGAGEMENT
(Susan Muska and Greta Olafsdottir, 2009)
This documentary covers how Edie Windsor fought the Defense of Marriage Act all the way up to the Supreme Court and won.

THE STRANGE HISTORY OF DON'T ASK, DON'T TELL
(Fenton Bailey and Randy Barbato, 2011)
A detailed look at the process of repealing the ban on gays and lesbians serving in the US military. Includes remarks from activists and politicians in addition to active and former service members.

BROTHER OUTSIDER: THE LIFE OF BAYARD RUSTIN
(Nancy D. Kates and Bennett Singer, 2003)
Chronicles Bayard Rustin, a Black gay man who was the organizer of the 1963 March on Washington where Martin Luther King Jr. famously gave his "I Have A Dream" speech.

COMMON THREADS: STORIES FROM THE QUILT
(Rob Epstein and Jeffrey Friedman, 1989)
Covers the first decade of the AIDS epidemic and the creation of the AIDS Memorial Quilt.

1 MEMORIAL MISSION

The AIDS Memorial Quilt is a beautiful memorial that helps educate people about HIV/AIDS while remembering the lives lost since cases were first reported. Visit the AIDS Memorial Quilt project website to learn about the history behind the quilt, the history of AIDS/HIV, and to learn where to visit an exhibition of the quilt. You could even ask your school, PTA, or GSA if they could host the quilt! Visit www.aidsmemorial.org

2 HEARING HISTORY

Find a podcast that educates you on a subject you'd like to learn and plan on listening to it once a week. You can even listen while doing another task! The MAKING GAY HISTORY podcast is a great option, with decades-old audio archives of the LGBTQ+ civil rights movement and personal portraits. makinggayhistory.com

3 ICONIC INTERVIEW

Contact your local LGBTQ+ center and ask to interview a queer person who was around during a significant historical time like the Stonewall Riots or AIDS epidemic to discover not only more about these moments in history, but a personal connection. If your interviewer is comfortable, take a photo or write a short story about what you learned to share online.

STRONGER TOGETHER

SELF QUEERY
QUEER QUESTIONS
WHAT IMPACT DOES QUEER EDUCATION HAVE ON SOCIETY?
ASK YOURSELF
QUEER QUESTIONS
WHAT TOOLS OR RESOURCES WILL YOU USE TO FILL IN YOUR EDUCATION GAPS?
ASK YOURSELF
QUEER QUESTIONS
WHAT DO YOU FEEL IS IMPORTANT FOR YOU TO LEARN IN ORDER TO BE SUCCESSFUL IN LIFE?
ASK YOURSELF
QUEER QUESTIONS
WHAT HAVE YOU NOT LEARNED IN SCHOOL THAT YOU ARE CURIOUS ABOUT?
ASK YOURSELF
CARE TO SHARE?
#ShareQueerCheer

RAINBOW AFFIRMATIONS

I am responsible for taking charge of my education.

I deserve a quality education, which includes learning about my community's history and culture.

I have the power to fight book bans and stand up to attempts to restrict my access to learning materials.

I help foster an environment of understanding by sharing knowledge of the queer community.

I am responsible for making sure I get a well-rounded education.

I am open to learning new things.

THE CATAGORY IS...

OUR COMMUNITY

One of the absolute best things about being queer is our community! Its history and impact on the world are something to dig into and be proud of! While some communities we live in can be challenging, when you find spots in this world where you can be true to you and flaunt your personality and interests with fellow queers, you'll discover a whole new sense of home, and trust. Our community has lots of welcoming spaces for you to sashay to!

NAVIGATING SPACES

You have a lot to offer this world. **You're wicked smart, talented, creative, and a total boss, with all that strength and resilience!** However, not everyone is as awesome as you. No shade, but some people out there are a hot mess, and they think dragging everyone else down makes them look better. Sometimes, they can make places unsafe, so keep your eyes peeled for any red flags. Wherever your scene may be, **watch for behavior or other peculiarities that sound the alarm and be prepared to hightail it into action.** Whether that means finding a sidekick, asking for help, or finding a safer place to be, prioritize your safety. Remember, you deserve respect wherever you go, and your self-value outranks the opinions of others. Don't let anyone else dim your shine!

"NEVER BE BULLIED INTO SILENCE. NEVER ALLOW YOURSELF TO BE MADE A VICTIM. ACCEPT NO ONE'S DEFINITION OF YOUR LIFE; DEFINE YOURSELF."
—HARVEY FIERSTEIN

Conversations On NAVIGATING SPACES

SHALOM (18)

"In all the spaces I engage in, I'm not the first queer person to be in them because queer people are everywhere. And so I'm not afraid. I don't feel pressured because I know that even if there's no queer people with me right in that moment, that a queer person has been there. Someone who's been in my shoes at some point in their life."

PERCY (18)

"Something I struggle with is getting misgendered in public. Navigating whether or not to use my birth name or chosen name in a situation can be stressful because sometimes I don't know if it is safe to be my full self or not. Other times it is just difficult to have to explain my identity all the time, so it is just easier to pretend to be my gender assigned at birth. Navigating how, when, and where it is safe and comfortable for me to pass is really difficult and it's something I'm still figuring out."

CHACE (17)

"I hung out with somebody, and we became relatively close friends. He came over to my house when there was somebody he knew to be queer there and he was upset that I was friends with that person. He ended up calling them a slur and I had to be like, 'You know that I'm queer too, right?' We ended up not being friends after that."

JACKIE (13)

"In middle school a family friend started teasing me for painting my nails and called me names like zesty. I was pretty sensitive about it. At the time, I was scared and didn't know what to do. My 'friend' kept calling me names when he had his other friends with him for protection. But one day when he was walking home alone, I went up to him and said, 'Are you going to shut up about that stuff?' He stopped calling me names after that. So, if you are facing oppression, stand up for yourself."

CONSTANCE (19)

"When I worked as a classroom aide, I identified as nonbinary, but I was pressured into publicly identifying as male so as to not "confuse the kids." After an HR complaint, I was allowed to breathe again, though. I managed by sticking up for myself and knowing my rights. Also by protecting my peace and not announcing my identity since I did not care what those people thought of me anyway."

LIS (17)

"Sometimes, when people say mean or negative things to me, I have to remind myself that everyone is allowed their own opinion. Many people will choose to be hurtful with their opinions, and that's obviously not okay for them to do. But I try to remember that what they think doesn't change who I am and what I believe in."

I CANNOT CONTROL

- What someone says or does
- How someone treats me
- Another's beliefs and opinions

I CAN CONTROL

- How I respond to and treat others
- How I let words affect me
- How I view and treat myself

HOW TO DEAL WITH BULLIES

1. Take a breath before reacting.
2. Stand up to bullies. Explain why their behavior is inappropriate.
3. Speak up to a trusted adult as soon as possible.
4. Travel with allies. Avoid negative people and unsafe places.
5. Remember that the problem is with the bully, not you.
6. Establish clear boundaries and rules for others to follow. Be firm.
7. Treat yourself with compassion and respect, and model this for others.

REMEMBER: Whether or not you choose to educate someone on their poor behavior, stereotypes, or ignorance, you are valid just as you are!

SPACE CHECK: WATCH FOR SIGNS, FLAGS, BEHAVIOR, CLOTHING, LANGUAGE, AND SYMBOLS THAT INDICATE TROUBLE. CHECK FOR ANTI-LGBTQ+ LAWS AND POLICIES.

INTERNET PEACE OF MIND

You don't have to engage with trolls or even read their messages/posts! It's okay to tune out social media or take a break. You don't need that negativity in your life!

WAYS TO IMPROVE ONLINE COMMUNITIES

- USE YOUR PLATFORM TO SHARE QUEER POSITIVITY
- MAKE CONNECTIONS WITH HELPFUL, ENCOURAGING, AND AFFIRMING PEOPLE
- ENGAGE IN UPLIFTING INTERACTIONS
- LIKE AND SHARE POSITIVE POSTS
- SEND MESSAGES OF LOVE, GRATITUDE, AND SUPPORT

Mute
Block
Report
Internet Bullies!

Try These ACTIVITIES

1 DESIGN YOUR OWN SANCTUARY

Create a place to be safe and away from fear. This could be your bedroom, the library, a park, or somewhere else you're comfortable being. Invite friends for a regular hangout.

2 SELF-DEFENSE

Take a self-defense class. Not only will this help you defend yourself against physical violence, but it can help you build confidence, too!

3 TOWN HALL

Go to your local town hall meeting and speak about your experience. Voice your concerns and ask for improvements to make your neighborhood a safer place.

STRONGER TOGETHER

SELF QUEERY
QUEER QUESTIONS
WHY DO YOU THINK PEOPLE DO OR SAY MEAN THINGS TO OTHERS?
ASK YOURSELF
QUEER QUESTIONS
WHAT IS ONE THING THAT COULD HELP YOU MANAGE A SPACE THAT IS NOT AS COMFORTABLE AS YOU DESIRE?
ASK YOURSELF
QUEER QUESTIONS
WHAT TYPES OF SIGNS, DECORATIONS, AND FLAGS ARE PRESENT IN YOUR NEIGHBORHOOD? WHAT TYPE OF CULTURE OR CLIMATE DO THEY SUGGEST?
ASK YOURSELF
QUEER QUESTIONS
WHAT IS SOMETHING POSITIVE YOU CAN SHARE ABOUT OUR COMMUNITY TO SOMEONE WHO HAS BEEN TOXIC OR NEGATIVE?
ASK YOURSELF
CARE TO SHARE?
#ShareQueerCheer

RAINBOW AFFIRMATIONS

I decide my level of visibility in every situation because I am the best judge of my own safety.

I am a valid member of my community and belong here just as much as anyone else.

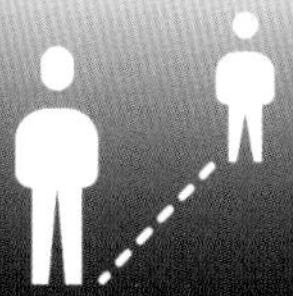

I have the right to distance myself from those who may cause me harm.

I have the ability to find spaces that are comfortable and respectful.

I believe in a future filled with spaces that celebrate and honor who I am.

I will not take other people's actions personally. I am amazing, and their behavior has nothing to do with me.

OUR FABULOUS CULTURE

You are part of a magnificent and wonderful culture filled with music, art, and love! **When it comes to entertainment, no one does it better than queer people.** We have drag kings and drag queens who entertain with humor, wit, and style. Queer singers regularly top the music charts, and we also have a major presence in Hollywood where many actors, directors, and screenwriters are part of the LGBTQ+ community. Think of your favorite movie or TV show. Chances are, somebody queer helped make it. **Our culture even has its own lingo**, fashion trends, various pride flags, special events such as pride parades, and so much more.

Ballroom culture, which originated among the Black and Latinx queer community in New York City, has had an incredible Influence on many things in our lives, including language, fashion, music, and more! You've probably heard of a popular dance style, voguing, which consists of runway poses emphasizing the arms and hands. That's right! Madonna's hit "Vogue" was inspired by queer people of color!

Conversations On OUR CULTURE

LUCY (19)

"POSE taught me a lot and just opened me up to learning more about the ballroom scene and the AIDS epidemic and stuff. That show is like a comfort show. Queer media can be really important, especially when it shares history and stuff."

SHALOM (18)

"I've been watching a lot of queer movies by people of color. There's one called PUNK, which is really good. It's the only Black queer rom-com that I found on the internet. I've been trying to create a collection of queer films featuring people of color. It's just great to see representation of that."

EVAN (18)

"I love drag; all the colors, outfits, and looks. It's fun to watch others perform in drag and I love doing it myself, too! Sometimes I'll dress up at home and do my own makeup. There's just so much expression involved. I didn't have many ways to express myself when I was younger and drag has definitely become an artistic outlet for me."

PERCY (18)

"I love that we have queer icons, people we see our queer identities represented in whether those people are queer or not. Like Dolly Parton. She's not queer, but she loves herself unapologetically, and that's something related to us: loving yourself unapologetically. Someone who embodies queer values."

CONSTANCE (19)

"Queer culture to me is ballroom. I could go on and on about it. I love how big a role trans women played in its founding, and the culture is so accepting and diverse. Queer culture changes, but ballroom is forever!"

CADENCE (13)

"My favorite band is Queen, and Freddie Mercury has been one of my idols for a long time, so when I found out he was part of the community, I thought it was really cool."

FAMOUS QUEER PEOPLE

A Few Past and Present Queer Icons Representing Our Fabulous Culture!

SINGERS

Lil Nas X
Sam Smith
Janelle Monáe
Lady Gaga
Kim Petras
Ricky Martin

ARTISTS

Leonardo da Vinci
Frida Kahlo
Michelangelo
Keith Haring
Andy Warhol
Francis Bacon

FASHION DESIGNERS

Giorgio Armani
Gianni Versace
Michael Kors
Jean Paul Gaultier
Hubert de Givenchy
Tom Ford

WRITERS

Oscar Wilde
James Baldwin
Alice Walker
Casey McQuiston
Malinda Lo
Aiden Thomas

ACTORS

Sir Ian McKellen
Noah Schnapp
Bella Ramsey
Elliot Page
Michaela Jaé Rodriguez
Tessa Thompson

1 PASSION FOR FASHION

Create your own fashion ensemble piece with clothes made or inspired by queer designers. Keep in mind, you can find fabulous treasures at secondhand stores. For extra fun, put on a ballroom contest with your friends. (Watch POSE for inspiration!)

2 QUEERAOKE

Find a list of queer musicians. Then grab a karaoke machine or use an app to throw a karaoke party where you and your friends sing their songs. Bonus points if you try out their dance moves!

3 MEDIA FOR THE MASSES

Start a film club or book club where you invite friends once a month to watch a movie or discuss a book by queer creators.

SELF QUEERY
QUEER QUESTIONS
WHAT IS ONE ASPECT OF QUEER HISTORY OR CULTURE THAT HAS INSPIRED YOU?
ASK YOURSE
QUEER QUESTIONS
WHAT ASPECT OF OUR CULTURE DO YOU RELATE TO THE MOST?
QUEER QUESTIONS
WHAT DO YOU BELIEVE YOUR GENERATION CONTRIBUTES TO QUEER CULTURE, AND WHAT LEGACY DO YOU THINK IT WILL LEAVE BEHIND?
ASK YOURSELF
CARE TO SHARE?
#ShareQueerCheer

RAINBOW AFFIRMATIONS

I am grateful for the abundance of queer culture, which provides endless opportunities for learning and connection.

As a member of the queer community, I contribute unique perspectives and ideas to the world.

Queer people have made significant contributions to society throughout history, and I am proud to be a part of this legacy.

I am grateful for the infinite inspiration and joy I can draw from queer culture.

Queer people are important and valuable members of society.

I draw strength from the legacy of resilient and courageous individuals who have come before me.

FINDING YOUR SPACE

The queer community is as diverse as the human race, and that's because queer people of every shape, size, color, ability, and origin are everywhere! And **if you're looking to find a place to belong within the queer community, all you need to do is look around.** From gaming to book clubs, there are a zillion combos of queer life filled with members of the community ready to geek out over shared interests. Try finding a group or activity by searching the internet, checking with your local LGBTQ+ centers, wandering through booths at a Pride festival, or asking a queer friend. And if you can't find a local group, start one yourself or create one online! You can totally foster the queer community of your dreams.

"I'VE BEEN EMBRACED BY A NEW COMMUNITY. THAT'S WHAT HAPPENS WHEN YOU'RE FINALLY HONEST ABOUT WHO YOU ARE: YOU FIND OTHERS LIKE YOU."
—CHAZ BONO

Conversations On FINDING YOUR SPACE

PERCY (18)

"You don't necessarily have to seek out queer people to find them. I've found people through shared interests like art and writing. I also love D&D and I've found a lot of other queer people love it too."

ADRIAN (19)

"I am studying vocal performance right now and plan on being a professional singer. Being queer in the arts has been great. I feel accepted and there is plenty of representation in my field."

CONSTANCE (19)

"My family moved when I was about sixteen and I had no community in my new town. But I did some research and found a local LGBTQ+ support group to attend which really helped! All of my friends are queer to some extent, so I have my own little community of people where we all uplift and help one another!"

SHALOM (18)

"Finding spaces for black queer men was comforting to me and really helpful with understanding my own identity and the reality of what it means to be a black queer person in this country and also the world."

JACKSON (18)

"I didn't really have a place to go physically to find community, especially since I couldn't drive. So, I went online. I found a lot of queer people I connected with on fanfiction sites."

NACEY (19)

"When I see another queer person it's like 'Ah, you get it!' It's so satisfying and so wonderful to have someone understand what you're thinking and help you talk through it."

WHAT'S YOUR PASSION?

Do you long to dance and sing among members of your community? Are you an athlete or musician looking to train with like-minded folx? Or do you simply want to share the joy of queer books with online friends? Check out this list for inspiration on where to find spaces that fit your personality.

EVENTS

Queer theme park days
Youth Pride events
Queer music concerts
Black Pride events
Queer movie nights
Pride marches
LGBTQ+ center youth events
Queer camp programs and events

CLUBS

Pride Leadership Academy
Queer Book Clubs
Queer Culture Club
Youth Art of Pride
Queer Women of Esports
UN's Queer Youth Dialogues
LGBTQ+ Teen Improv Theatre
Queer ballroom dancing
Front Runners
Youth Pride Marching Band
AIDS LifeCycle
Queer Youth Chorus

Did you know the NYC Pride March is consistently North America's biggest Pride parade? In 2019, they had an estimated four million in attendance for the parade and an estimated five million taking part over Pride weekend.

Try These ACTIVITIES

1 MAKE A MATCH

Make a list of two to three hobbies, then contact your local LGBTQ+ center to see if they have any groups you are interested in participating in. Consider virtual options too! Check online sources for virtual chats, gaming groups, and more. Keep internet safety in mind and never give out your personal information. Also, report online harassment if you witness it.

2 PRIDE EVENTS

Attend a Pride parade or celebration. This is a great opportunity to be around other queer people and find out about other queer events. Maybe you'll learn about a new club or another place to meet like-minded people.

3 WEAR YOUR FLAIR

If you're a bit shy, try wearing or displaying your personality and interests on your clothing, backpack, or books. Maybe even wear something Pride-related, like rainbow flags or pins. When someone comments on them, it gives you a chance to chat and perhaps ask if they have a group you can join.

STRONGER TOGETHER

SELF QUEERY
QUEER QUESTIONS
HOW DOES BELONGING DIFFER FROM MERELY FITTING IN? DO SHARED VALUES, INTERESTS, AND ACCEPTANCE PLAY A ROLE?
ASK YOURSELF
QUEER QUESTIONS
WHAT DO YOU THINK A COMMUNITY OFFERS? WHAT DO YOU HOPE TO GAIN FROM BEING PART OF ONE?
QUEER QUESTIONS
WHAT IS ONE ASPECT OF THE QUEER COMMUNITY THAT YOU ARE CURIOUS ABOUT OR OPEN TO EXPLORING?
ASK YOURSELF
QUEER QUESTIONS
DO YOU ADAPT TO DIFFERENT VERSIONS OF YOURSELF IN DIFFERENT SPACES, OR CAN YOU ALWAYS BE YOUR TRUE SELF? WHY?
ASK YOURSELF
CARE TO SHARE?
#ShareQueerCheer

RAINBOW AFFIRMATIONS

I am dedicated to creating a space where everyone can feel a sense of belonging and acceptance.

I am dedicated to being a part of a community where I can connect and relate with like-minded individuals.

I can find a community where I can be myself and find acceptance and fulfillment.

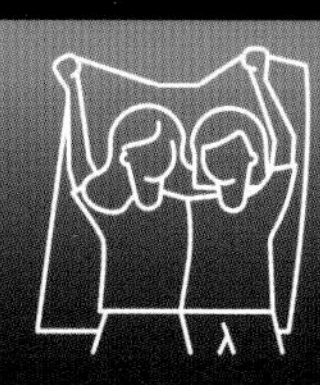

I embrace and celebrate the unique diversity of my community.

By being my true, authentic self, I can create an environment of acceptance and belonging for others around me.

I choose to surround myself with people who appreciate and value me for who I am.

SUPPORTING OUR COMMUNITY

One of the best things about the queer community is that we have each other's backs. You can see examples of this by looking at all the services provided by LGBTQ+ centers across the country. They offer support groups, health services, safe spaces, and more! Many in our community volunteer at these and other nonprofits that focus on giving trans-affirming care, emergency housing for queer teens, and support for the queer community. **Whether you're looking to clock some community service hours, or you dream of making a difference, you can't go wrong with giving your time and talents to these organizations.** Or, if you're all about a cause, like fighting bigotry, saving the environment, or rescuing animals, you can volunteer with an organization that matches your vibe. However you decide to give back, not only will your efforts be totally appreciated, but you might pick up some new skills and find like-minded friends!

WE TAKE CARE OF OUR OWN

Did you know that when the AIDS epidemic first started, and was decimating gay and bisexual men, many doctors were too scared to even go into the hospital rooms to give medical attention to the patients? It was queer women who stepped in to take care of men dying of AIDS when no one else would.

Conversations On

SUPPORTING OUR COMMUNITY

CONSTANCE (19)

"Always stick up for the underdog. If you see somebody alone and struggling, talk to them. It helps so much just to have somebody listen to you. You don't necessarily have to give yourself to them or become their friend. Just let them know that they're a person on this Earth just like everyone else is."

CHACE (17)

"We organized a Pride parade. We also had a pretty significant presence at local Pride meetups like a Pride gift swap where people would make crafts and trade art with people. I helped one of my friends wood-burn a bunch of little discs to give away."

NACEY (19)

"I volunteered at Pride Fest in Chicago my sophomore and senior year, and I'm doing it again this month. I also helped set up Pride in the Park and passed out flyers to people walking in wanting to donate. It was fun and made me feel like a part of something. It opened up my eyes to a big queer community and it made me feel more okay with myself."

POTENTIAL BENEFITS OF VOLUNTEERING

INCREASES SOCIALIZATION
Reduces loneliness and isolation by connecting people

STRENGTHENS RELATIONSHIPS
Volunteering with family and friends strengthens bonds

PROVIDES CAREER DIRECTION
Try a career and gain experience without long-term commitment

STRENGTHENS COMMUNITIES
Volunteers can unite to address community challenges

IMPROVES SELF-ESTEEM
Boosts confidence and fosters pride and accomplishment

BUILDS RESUME AND COLLEGE APPLICATION
Learn skills like teamwork and project management

INCREASES HAPPINESS
Helping others can feel good

"When you put love out in the world it travels, and it can touch people and reach people in ways that we never even expected."
—Laverne Cox

1 OBSERVE YOUR COMMUNITY'S NEEDS

Spend a day at your local LGBTQ+ center, or somewhere in our community, and observe and talk with people. Can you name the community's needs and find a unique solution for one?

2 KINDNESS CHALLENGE

Search for a kindness challenge online where you challenge yourself to one act of kindness a day. Do this for a week, a month, or for however long you choose.

3 VOLUNTEER FOR A DAY

Contact your local LGBTQ+ center to see if there are ways you can volunteer within the community. You could also search Dosomething.org (a youth volunteer website) for a cause that speaks to you. Sign up to volunteer or take action!

STRONGER TOGETHER

SELF QUEERY
QUEER QUESTIONS
WHICH GLOBAL OR COMMUNITY ISSUES CONCERN YOU THE MOST, AND HOW CAN YOU CONTRIBUTE TO THE SOLUTIONS?
ASK YOURSELF
QUEER QUESTIONS
WHAT SKILLS DO YOU POSSESS THAT COULD BE HELPFUL TO THE COMMUNITY?
ASK YOURSELF
QUEER QUESTIONS
WHAT NEEDS DO YOU THINK THE QUEER COMMUNITY HAS?
ASK YOURSELF
QUEER QUESTIONS
WHAT ARE SOME THINGS YOU COULD GAIN OR LEARN BY VOLUNTEERING WITH A NONPROFIT ORGANIZATION? ARE THERE ANY DOWNSIDES TO THE COMMITMENT?
ASK YOURSELF
CARE TO SHARE?
#ShareQueerCheer

RAINBOW AFFIRMATIONS

I have the opportunity to be an inspiration to those going through the same struggles as me.

I choose to empower my community to create meaningful connections and inspire positive change.

I can offer my time, knowledge, and energy to help those who are in need.

I give freely without expecting anything in return.

I make a big difference every time I give to a good cause.

It is okay to say no, and to only volunteer in ways that do not require me to overextend myself.

ACTIVISM

Activism and civil disobedience are deeply intertwined with queer culture. **Throughout history, many amazing people in our community have stood up and created positive change.** From Stonewall to marriage equality and beyond. We've made a lot of progress with LGBTQ+ equality over the years, and while we've also had a few setbacks with laws targeting our community, our successes far outnumber our losses. We've been able to win and fight back because our community banded together with allies and took action. Is there a law or policy you disagree with? **Voting is the most important thing you can do to create change in the political system so make sure you're registered when you're eligible.** But even if you're not old enough to vote, there are still many ways you can make a huge impact! Just take a look at what some of these amazing teens have done!

A few examples of queer activism from history include the Stonewall uprising, where queer people fought back against police harassment; ACT UP, a grassroots political organization that fought to draw attention to the AIDS epidemic; and the 1993 March on Washington, where an estimated one million people protested for equal rights.

Conversations On ACTIVISM

LUCY (19)

"I was a social media manager for a coalition trying to lower the voting age in Hawaii to sixteen. I was also involved with the Keiki Caucus in Hawaii, where we worked on bills for youth that we wanted to see get passed in the legislature. Through that, I submitted testimony on a bathroom bill and an education bill. I was also the outreach director for the Hawai'i Youth Climate Coalition, where we tried to make environmental spaces inclusive."

NACEY (19)

"During BLM, I remember going out and protesting in Chicago, and on social media I was helping petitions get passed. That was the first time I was ever involved in activism. I also went to community centers where we could all talk about things and educate each other. That was really helpful in understanding what was going on."

CHACE (17)

"I helped a group start a petition for a bill being debated in my state legislature which was whether or not the state would allow undocumented people to get driver's licenses and be able to operate vehicles legally in Rhode Island. And in part due to our activism the bill was signed into law, which was really exciting for us eleventh graders."

CONSTANCE (19)

"When my friend was involved in a school shooting, I really woke up and realized I can't just say I'm an ally, I actually have to act as one. So I made calls to representatives and donated money I'd saved up by teaching piano lessons so I could contribute to change in the world."

SHALOM (18)

"I met with the Pan African Community Alliance to talk about ways we can actively create better leadership within the Black community. I'm also president and founder of CSUN's Queer Students of Color club, which is an affinity space for Queer POC to express themselves and find community outside of the predominantly white queer spaces that were already established. In 2020, I also sang to help my school raise $3,600 for the Marsha P. Johnson Institute."

Conversations On ACTIVISM

SHALOM (18)

"Art is the most peaceful yet aggressive form of protest because of the way that art can permeate the mind. Like, a song can fundamentally change the way someone sees the world. It's just so powerful. Sometimes people don't even realize they're learning when they interact with art, but it's a form of cultural exchange. When it comes to activism, art is the best way for underage people to go."

LUCY (19)

"Being involved in activism provided me a deeper understanding of how things work, why things are the way that they are, and the intentionality behind things. It also provided a community that was cool to be a part of, because it was like-minded individuals who really cared about the world and other people. It was life-changing."

ALIA (17)

"I think it's very important that young people are in leadership roles—especially when it's us being attacked. Having our voices be heard and having conversations with us. If you do choose to be involved with advocacy, you kind of claim your power with that. I may be a young person, but that doesn't reduce my power."

LUKE (16)

"Just because we can't vote doesn't mean we can't still have a voice. Our voices are very loud and all it takes to see change is to speak out. Push peer pressure and the fear of being rejected to the side and speak up."

JACKIE (13)

"Just you standing up can make one person stop and be like, 'Hey, maybe I should stand with this person against oppression because it's wrong,' and then it starts building up and up and soon this community of thousands of people is formed, and it's wonderful."

CONSTANCE (19)

"Anti-LGBTQ bills motivate me to put my art into the world so I can change it for the better. It definitely feels despairing at times, but things won't always be like this. Not if I can do anything about it."

MAKE A DIFFERENCE

Just because someone is not old enough to vote, doesn't mean they can't create positive changes in their communities. Here are a few ways to get involved.

GET PEOPLE REGISTERED TO VOTE	SHARE YOUR OPINION WITH VOTERS	PROVIDE PRE-FILLED POSTCARDS TO LEGISLATORS FOR PEOPLE TO SIGN	CONTACT YOUR LOCAL POLITICIAN
ORGANIZE OR ATTEND A PROTEST RALLY	USE ART TO CREATE AWARENESS	VOLUNTEER IN YOUR LOCAL POLITICIAN'S OFFICE	PASS OUT FLYERS
HELP EDUCATE THE PUBLIC BY PHONE BANKING	SHARE YOUR STORY BY SPEAKING AT LOCAL EVENTS, CENTERS, OR SCHOOLS	POST, SHARE, AND COMMENT ABOUT IMPORTANT ISSUES ON SOCIAL MEDIA	CREATE PETITIONS OR GET SUPPORT FOR EXISTING PETITIONS
WRITE AN ARTICLE OR GET THE PRESS INVOLVED	TAKE PHOTOS OR VIDEOS TO SHARE	JOIN OR FORM A SOCIAL JUSTICE/ COMMUNITY CHANGE CLUB	WRITE LETTERS TO COMPANIES OR POLITICIANS

"WE NEED, IN EVERY COMMUNITY, A GROUP OF ANGELIC TROUBLEMAKERS." —BAYARD RUSTIN

IS IT FAKE NEWS?

SOMETIMES, CURRENT EVENTS CAN MOTIVATE US TO WORK FOR POSITIVE CHANGE, BUT, BEFORE YOU TAKE ACTION, ENSURE YOUR INFORMATION IS ACCURATE.

CHECK THE SOURCE
If the source is unfamiliar, investigate its credibility, mission, and contact info. Look for grammar or website errors.

READ BEYOND THE HEADLINE
Some headlines are misleading. Read the whole story to get more information.

CHECK THE AUTHOR
Research authors to determine expertise, credibility, motivation, and if they are even real.

KEEP A CRITICAL MINDSET
Question the purpose of a story, checking for bias or emotional manipulation, even if it's a trusted source.

VERIFY SUPPORTING EVIDENCE
Credible sources include trustworthy data, statistics, and quotes from experts to back up their reporting. If these things are missing, ask why.

FACT CHECK
Use fact-checking sites like Snopes for more information.

CHECK THE DATE
Verify the information is current. Old news is not necessarily relevant to current events.

VERIFY IMAGES AND VIDEOS
Images and videos could have been edited, manipulated, created by A.I., or used out of context to mislead. Use tools like Google's Reverse Image Search to verify authenticity.

IS IT A JOKE?
Does the story sound off or outlandish? Verify it's not a joke or posted on a satire website like THE ONION.

CHECK YOUR BIASES
Diversify sources to get different perspectives and facts and to counter the confirmation bias of echo chambers created by social media and browser history.

CHECK OTHER SOURCES
If it sounds like a big story and no other major news outlet is reporting it, use caution.

1 ACTIVISM ART

Use art as a catalyst for change by creating a sign, taking a photo, or making a piece of art that can inspire activism. Display it somewhere publicly.

2 EMAIL EXPRESSIONS

Speak up by writing an email or letter to your local politician, expressing why an issue is important to you and what actions you expect them to take.

3 ELECTION READY

Prepare for voting by pre-registering or registering to vote and keeping yourself updated on upcoming elections. You can even volunteer in an election to learn more about how it works.

STRONGER TOGETHER

SELF QUEERY
QUEER QUESTIONS
HAVE YOU EVER STOOD UP FOR SOMETHING YOU THOUGHT WAS RIGHT? WHAT WAS IT?
ASK YOURSELF
QUEER QUESTIONS
ARE THERE LAWS YOU DISAGREE WITH? WHAT ARE THEY, AND HOW CAN YOU IMPACT CHANGE?
QUEER QUESTIONS
ARE THERE OTHER GROUPS YOU CAN WORK WITH TO ACHIEVE A COMMON GOAL?
ASK YOURSELF
QUEER QUESTIONS
ARE ANY OF YOUR VALUES OR DECISIONS SHAPED BY POLITICS? WHY OR WHY NOT?
ASK YOURSELF
CARE TO SHARE?
#ShareQueerCheer

RAINBOW AFFIRMATIONS

I am determined to make positive changes for my community. Giving up is not an option.

I can raise my voice to protect my freedoms.

I surround myself with allies who share common goals.

My efforts, both big and small, are important and valuable.

I will not compromise my principles to please those who oppose me.

I am confident in my abilities and talents to improve the present state of the world.

THE CATAGORY IS... SUCCESS & FUTURE

Your future may seem like a long way off, but it's never too early to start planning! Whether it's a cross-country road trip, becoming a CEO, admission to that cool inclusive college, marrying the person of your dreams, or starting your own family, you can do it! Every step you take today can help shape the path ahead of you. As a queer teen, things may feel challenging at times, but there's plenty of support and inspiration if you seek it. Setting goals throughout life will not only shape your future but also help you maintain a positive outlook. With the right mindset, planning, and support, you can overcome any obstacle and achieve your biggest dreams.

Queer people can do amazing things!

DREAM IT, BE IT

What are your plans for the future? Do you want to go to college? Maybe travel? Start a family? Or maybe all of the above! **If you don't know exactly what you want to do, or where you want to be in the future, that's okay!** Start with exploring possibilities or jot down a few simple dreams. Perhaps you can talk to your school counselor, attend a job fair, pick up a career-finder book, or ask to shadow successful people whose lives you admire. **You don't have to have your entire future nailed down right now, but it's important to know you can be successful AND happy!** There are limitless opportunities ahead for you. All you have to do is reach up and start grabbing! Now slay the future runway!

"I'M A LIVING WITNESS THAT DREAMS DO COME TRUE, EVEN IF THEY AREN'T THE ONES YOU START OUT WITH." —BILLY PORTER

Conversations On DREAMS

NACEY (19)

"If I could turn sailing into a real job, that would be my dream."

JACKIE (13)

"I want to be a dad 100 percent because I'm really connected to both of my parents, and if I end up having kids, having that same experience with them would be amazing. Today there are plenty of options, and it's great to know that I can still have kids even if I marry a man."

JACKSON (18)

"I'm going to college and studying gender studies. At least for now. Also, I really enjoy cutting and dyeing hair, so I'm considering become a hairdresser."

EVAN (18)

"My boyfriend and I have talked about marriage and starting a family together in the future. I want to wait a while before having kids, though, to make sure I have my life together."

SHALOM (18)

"I wanna make a cartoon with music in it. I really want to create something for queer kids that shows the reality of being queer. I also want to do entertainment law and I wanna open a little cafe when I'm old."

LUCY (19)

"I'd like to get a degree that's relevant to environmental policy. My dream job would be an environmental educator at a national park. I'd also like to travel. I think that provides a lot of understanding of the world."

ADRIAN (19)

"My goal is to tour with my own music and band. I would also like to marry eventually! I only hesitate with having kids because I don't want them to struggle in this world. As a queer, Latina woman, I know there are many injustices my kids could face, and I want to protect them from that. On the other hand, I would love to have a family and support my children."

CHACE (17)

"I am double majoring in computer science and engineering with a minor in math. Because I am actually insane. A college teacher told me that the average college major changes their major about five times. I am so ready to get closer and closer to that average if need be."

CALLAHAN (18)

"I consume a lot of content on social media about trans men getting married, having jobs, and things like that. It's inspiring because I see trans people who have achieved their dreams and are successful. It lets me know that I can achieve my dreams and goals as well."

PARKER (16)

"I have the opportunity to graduate early because of my alternative school, and then I want to go to college for culinary arts. I want to own my own bakery or restaurant. That would be really cool."

COMPANIES THAT HAVE HAD OPENLY LGBTQ+ LEADERS

Did you know that some of the top companies in the world have been run by people who were openly queer? It's true! Here are a few examples.

AmeriCorps—Michael D. Smith, CEO
Apple, Inc.—Tim Cook, CEO
Coty—Sue Nabi, CEO
Dow Chemicals—Jim Fitterling, CEO
Fidelity International—Anne Richards, CEO
Golden State Warriors NBA—Rick Welts, president and COO
Land O'Lakes—Beth Ford, CEO
Macy's—Jeffrey Gennette, CEO
Qantas Airways—Alan Joyce, CEO
United Therapeutics—Martine Rothblatt, CEO

"I made a decision long ago to live an authentic life, and if my being named CEO helps others do the same, that's a wonderful moment."
—Land O'Lakes's Beth Ford in 2018, the same year she became the first openly gay woman to lead a Fortune 500 company.

Jeffrey Gennette has been out professionally since his first day at Macy's on July 5, 1983. He rose through the ranks, becoming president in 2014, despite being warned that being openly gay could hinder his career.

LGBTQ+ CAREER TRAILBLAZERS

Many LGBTQ+ individuals have excelled in career fields across the spectrum! Here are just a few shining stars.

Music: Stephen Sondheim—Gay American composer who majorly influenced the musical theater scene; he has won eight Tony Awards.

Politics: Tammy Baldwin—Lesbian Wisconsin Senator who became the first openly LGBTQ+ Senator and the first openly LGBTQ+ politician elected as a US Representative.

Psychology: Dr. John Ercel Fryer—Gay psychiatrist whose American Psychiatric Association speech was key in removing homosexuality as a mental disorder.

Literature: Alice Walker—Bisexual African American author and the first Black woman to win the Pulitzer Prize for her book, THE COLOR PURPLE.

Math/Computer Science: Alan Turing—Gay British mathematician and computer scientist whose codebreaking saved countless lives during World War II.

Sports: Jason Collins—Pro basketball player and first active, openly gay male athlete to play in any of the four major US pro sports leagues (NBA, NFL, MLB or NHL).

Military: Lt. Col. Bree Fram—Out, trans, active-duty US Space Force astronautical engineer leading space policy integration at the Pentagon.

Business: Tim Cook—CEO of Apple Inc. and the first Fortune 500 chief executive to identify publicly as a gay man.

Judicial: Mary Yu—Washington Supreme Court's first Latina, first Asian-American, and first openly gay justice.

1 THE THREE BUCKETS

A bucket list is a list of experiences or achievements a person wants to have in their lifetime. In this activity, let's create three "buckets" (or lists): one for things you want to do in the next year, one for things you want to do in the next five years, and finally, a lifetime achievement list. Then choose one item from each list and create a plan.

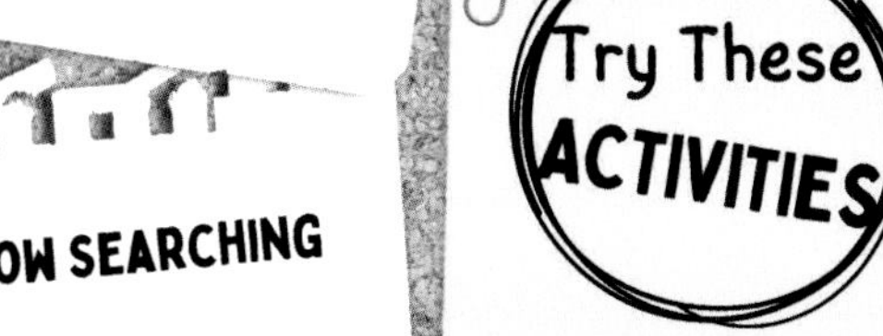

2 SHADOW SEARCHING

Shadow people in various career fields (ask an adult to help line up opportunities if needed). Try a few options you're interested in, as well as ones you haven't considered. It could be an assistant, banker, electrician, musician, chef, law clerk —anything you're curious about! Ruling out a career is a step toward finding the right one!

3 INSPIRATION STATION

Hobbies we enjoy are often overlooked as career possibilities. Try this! List your hobbies and activities. Now brainstorm career ideas or search the web for how others have turned this into a career! Bonus: Pick up the book WHAT COLOR IS MY PARACHUTE to take a career assessment test and discover possibilities based on your talents.

SELF QUEERY
QUEER QUESTIONS
WHAT'S SOMETHING IN THE FUTURE THAT YOU'RE EXCITED ABOUT?
ASK YOURSELF
QUEER QUESTIONS
WHAT OPTIONS HAVE YOU CONSIDERED TAKING ONCE YOU FINISH SCHOOL, BEYOND YOUR CAREER?
ASK YOURSELF
QUEER QUESTIONS
WHAT ARE SOME THINGS YOU WANT TO GET BETTER AT DOING?
ASK YOURSELF
QUEER QUESTIONS
WHAT ARE SOME THINGS YOU LOVE THAT YOU WISH YOU DID MORE OFTEN? HOW COULD YOU INCORPORATE THESE IN YOUR PLANS?
ASK YOURSELF
CARE TO SHARE?
#ShareQueerCheer

RAINBOW AFFIRMATIONS

I have the ability to create my own destiny.

I can be out, happy, and successful in the career I choose.

I possess the qualities I need to be successful in life.

My life is more than the money I make, the car I drive, the house I live in, or the career I choose.

I am allowed to change my direction at any time.

I am allowed to take my time to explore my possibilities and pick a path that makes me happy.

ACHIEVING GOALS

Making progress in life requires more than just dreaming, you have to dig in and work! While dreaming is important, setting goals helps you actively work toward achieving your aspirations. Planning your path to success by mapping out goals can help keep you focused on achieving your dreams, provide clarity in decision making, help manage expectations, and keep you motivated during setbacks.

If a goal feels overwhelming, try breaking it up into smaller tasks. You can even try out different methods to motivate and inspire you. With persistence and determination, you will find a way to stay on track toward completing your goals. This will not only help you achieve more, but also give you a sense of accomplishment and fulfillment. So, go ahead, reach for the stars, and don't forget to celebrate your milestones along the way!

"IF YOU FEEL LIKE THERE'S SOMETHING OUT THERE THAT YOU'RE SUPPOSED TO BE DOING, IF YOU HAVE A PASSION FOR IT, THEN STOP WISHING AND JUST DO IT."
—WANDA SYKES

Conversations On ACHIEVING GOALS

LUCY (19)

"Writing down goals and talking about them is really important because it makes them more of a reality. And I think including people in on your goals can be important."

CHACE (17)

"When I really need to sit down and focus on something, I'll set a timer and then I'll look down at whatever I'm doing and really kind of crank it out until I kind of break or I'm not paying attention. I'll stop the timer and it's like, 'Oh, I got fifteen minutes. I wonder if I can do twenty next time!' "

SHALOM (18)

"I have ADHD, and so my best tool is an agenda book to make sure I have my schedule written out and making sure that there's someone who checks in with me. Then also making sure I have like a realistic and clear plan."

PERCY (18)

"Having a visual representation of my goals can really help me, whether that be in the form of a list, a diagram, or drawing. Having something I can revisit at a future time to check my progress is really helpful."

ADARA (18)

"I have a list of things that sometimes work if I really need to get something done. On my list: Watch a videogame walkthrough, use an app with a timer for productivity, move to a different location to work on stuff, and something I particularly find that works is body doubling, where someone else is in the room."

PARKER (16)

"I'll try to do the most exhausting and boring task first. Which always seems to be the dishes. I despise doing dishes. I'll separate tasks that I know I have to get done or that I know will take up the most time. It helps to plan when certain tasks will take longer or must be done on a certain day."

CONSTANCE (19)

"I usually have an accountability buddy—someone who can check in with me and hold me accountable for when I'm slacking off or procrastinating. I set deadlines for myself and work together with my accountability buddy to make sure it gets done."

ACHIEVE YOUR GOALS

Looking for guidance in reaching your goals? Check out these tips to help you stay motivated and organized while pursuing your dreams!

- Write down your goals with deadlines
- Break goals into smaller, manageable tasks
- Analyze time requirements
- Take time each week to schedule tasks
- Schedule priority tasks first
- Plan remaining tasks if time allows
- Remember to plan time for self-care!
- Reassess and address roadblocks as needed
- Remind yourself of a goal's importance as you go
- Give yourself grace to learn and adjust
- Check off tasks when complete
- Reward yourself each time you meet a milestone

1 ACCOUNTABLE ALLIES

Find a trusted friend or group. Discuss your intentions with them and establish a consistent time to check in when you can discuss your progress, offer encouragement, and provide feedback. You can even try body doubling sessions, in which they work alongside you virtually or in person while you complete your tasks.

2 MAPP IT

Try downloading a goal tracking app and map out a few of your short-term goals. Use it regularly for a month and then evaluate whether or not it was beneficial for you. Was it easy to use? Did it help you stay on track? Did it help you successfully achieve your goal?

3 VISUALIZE IT

Make a visual representation of your bucket list, hopes, and dreams by pasting or drawing pictures and words onto a poster board. You can cut from a magazine, use stickers, draw on it, or glitter it up! You can even go digital and use Pinterest, Canva, or other apps.

SELF QUEERY
QUEER QUESTIONS
HOW DO YOU DEFINE FAILURE? HOW ABOUT SUCCESS?
ASK YOURSELF
QUEER QUESTIONS
WHEN IS IT OKAY TO GIVE UP ON A GOAL?
QUEER QUESTIONS
WHAT IS YOUR NUMBER ONE GOAL RIGHT NOW?
ASK YOURSELF
QUEER QUESTIONS
WHAT WOULD MAKE YOU FEEL MORE SUPPORTED IN ACHIEVING YOUR GOALS?
ASK YOURSELF
CARE TO SHARE?
#ShareQueerCheer

RAINBOW AFFIRMATIONS

I set great goals and work hard to achieve them.

I can do anything if I put my mind to it.

I will take one step forward today, no matter how small.

I recognize and celebrate what I have achieved.

I can realize my potential for success by remembering how far I've come.

I am focused and ready to give my best today.

GROWTH MINDSET

Have you ever learned from a mistake or epically failed at something only to come out stronger on the other side? That's a growth mindset! It's when you **take the opportunity to turn failures into a springboard for personal growth.** Anyone can change and grow through their own efforts and experiences. Harvey Milk, one of our most celebrated queer icons, is the perfect example of this. He lost his campaign for public office three times before finally winning! After each loss, he reevaluated his campaign strategy and identified ways he could improve his community, meet more voters, and ultimately win more votes. He smashed through all obstacles, learning how to succeed where previously no other openly gay male candidate had before. Let Harvey's story inspire you to succeed through a growth mindset! **Resist the urge to compare yourself to others, and remember that setbacks aren't roadblocks, they're part of your journey.** If you view your setbacks as opportunities to learn, you'll be in a better position to develop your skills, boost your confidence, and increase your chances of future success!

"EXPERIENCE IS SIMPLY THE NAME WE GIVE OUR MISTAKES."
—OSCAR WILDE

Conversations On GROWTH MINDSET

CHACE (17)

"I wrote this hilariously bad paper for one of my classes and I went and I talked to one of my teachers about it. He taught me how to write way better than I already could and because of that I was actually gifted best in class for writing and scouted as an English tutor for a job. And that's something that would absolutely never have happened if I didn't write that garbage paper."

LUKE (16)

"I always like looking back at past experiences, even if they were bad, and looking at how I can change the way that I do things and what can I do moving forward to improve how I'm looking at things. And I think that hindsight is really, really helpful. Everything is a learning experience. Everything happens for a reason, and you always learn and grow."

ADRIAN (19)

"I had a goal to put music out a few years ago. I recorded some music that didn't feel like my best work. I learned not to push my limits too far and to allow myself grace to come up with something that feels authentic."

CONSTANCE (19)

"When I was fifteen, I tried to direct an entire play by myself. After most of the cast quit, I switched to a play that needed less people, and when they quit I redirected myself to helping my high school's theater company by teaching music. I'm glad I didn't give up and was able to do something theater-related in the end."

PARKER (16)

"In cooking, sometimes it's not right the first time. When I've never made something before, it can take two or three tries. In cooking you throw stuff together and hope it works. And if it doesn't, you just figure out what you can or can't add to it to make it better. I learned that if something's too salty, you can use potatoes to absorb the salt."

STEPS ON DEALING WITH FAILURE

Give yourself permission to fail.

Give yourself compassion. (Failure is not your identity!)

Try not to place blame.

Look at it from a different perspective.

Reflect on what can be learned.

Don't dwell on the failure.

Review your goals and plan for the future.

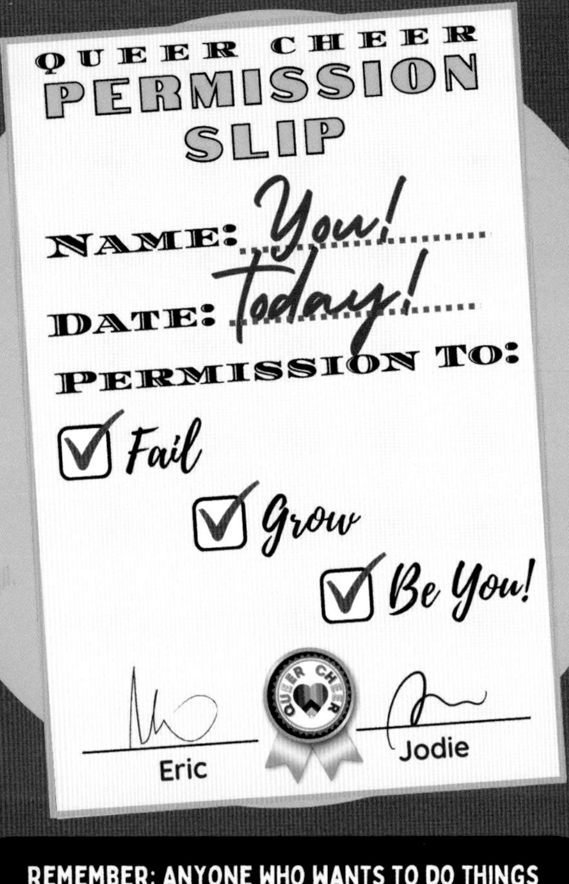

QUEER CHEER
PERMISSION SLIP

NAME: *You!*

DATE: *today!*

PERMISSION TO:

- [x] *Fail*
- [x] *Grow*
- [x] *Be You!*

Eric — QUEER CHEER — Jodie

REMEMBER: ANYONE WHO WANTS TO DO THINGS OF VALUE IN LIFE WILL FAIL AND MAKE MISTAKES.

1 GET INSPIRED

Watch the film MILK to learn how this incredible queer icon used growth mindset. How did he progress and learn from his failures?

2 EXAMINE YOUR ACHIEVEMENTS

List your achievements, then think of what you did to get them. Can you identify struggles or failures in your path to those achievements in which you learned something new or found a way to overcome?

3 EXAMINE A GOAL

Write down a goal, then create two lists: 1) The barriers you have to achieving that goal. 2) The fears holding you back from achieving that goal. Examine your lists. How are those fears and barriers connected? Can you brainstorm a way to work past these barriers?

STRONGER TOGETHER

SELF QUEERY
QUEER QUESTIONS
IN WHAT WAYS HAVE YOU GROWN OVER THE LAST YEAR? WHAT HELPED YOU GET THERE?
ASK YOURSELF
QUEER QUESTIONS
IN WHAT WAYS DO YOU STRUGGLE WITH PERFECTIONISM?
ASK YOURSELF
QUEER QUESTIONS
WHAT IS A DIFFERENT STRATEGY YOU COULD USE FOR A PROBLEM YOU'RE FACING?
ASK YOURSELF
QUEER QUESTIONS
WHO CAN YOU ASK FOR HONEST FEEDBACK ON YOUR EFFORTS?
ASK YOURSELF
CARE TO SHARE?
#ShareQueerCheer

RAINBOW AFFIRMATIONS

I strive for progress, not perfection. No one is perfect.

I embrace challenges. They help me learn and grow stronger.

Just because I am struggling does not mean I am failing.

I will remain patient and diligent, as all great things take effort and time.

I have the ability to find learning opportunities within my mistakes.

My mistakes do not define me.

Congratulations! You did it!

You made it to the end of this book, and look how far you've come. You've stretched yourself emotionally, stepped outside of your comfort zone, and dug deep inside to reflect on who you are as a person. And guess what? You're an AMAZING human being! Don't ever forget that. You're a VIP, baby!

So, now comes the exciting part—living the rest of your life to the fullest! You have so many wonderful adventures ahead of you, and you'll meet magnificent people along the way. There's so much love, support, friendship, acceptance, and success out there. You will find it and it will find you.

If you ever find yourself doubting your brilliance, or maybe you just feel like there's an area you need to work on more, come back to this book and revisit that section again because we're always here to cheer you on. And if you want to share positive messages or encouraging stories to help inspire other teens just like you, post online with #ShareQueerCheer. You have the power to lift others up and spread positivity across our amazing community!

Now, before you close this book and step back out into the world, remember to adjust your crown, aim high, and be bold, because you are fierce. You are sickening. You are unstoppable! This is your moment, and the world is your runway. So, go out there, live loud and proud, and don't forget to spread some Queer Cheer along the way!

Love always!
Eric & Jodie

LGBTQ+ RESOURCES

For additional resources and content, visit CheerQueerBook.com. You may also find resources at your local LGBTQ+ center. Find one at lgbtqcenters.org or search online.

For free internet access, consider visiting your local library, LGBTQ+ center, or trusted public Wi-Fi locations. You might also qualify for local or government programs that offer free or discounted internet and laptop programs.

ADVOCACY, INCLUSION & EQUALITY SUPPORT

Athlete Ally
Promotes inclusion in sports. Has a database of LGBTQ+ policies and practices for all levels of institutions and conferences.
AthleteAlly.org (646) 389-0225

GLAAD
Advocates for LGBTQ+ acceptance. Programs for Spirit Day, resources for social media safety, media accountability, global voices, Black creators, gamers, and HIV+.
GLAAD.org

InterACT
Advocates for Intersex Youth
A youth program that includes resource topics, brochures, guides, and lists of intersex policies, support groups, and advocacy groups.
InteractAdvocates.org
(707) 793-1190

National Center for Transgender Equality
Information on transgender rights in employment, military, schools, etc. Guides and resources for health coverage, name changes, ID documents, and legal services.
TransEquality.org (202) 642-4542

Parents, Families, and Friends of Lesbians and Gays (PFLAG)
Provides in-person and virtual peer support, intersectional community connection, workshops, story sharing, faith-based support, and more.
pflag.org (202) 467-8180

CRISIS AND SUPPORT LINES (FREE AND CONFIDENTIAL)

988 Suicide & Crisis Lifeline
24/7 LGBTQ+ counseling. Also has stories of hope and recovery, safety plans, and resources for services and community connection.
988lifeline.org (Click LGBTQ+)
Text "Q" to 988 or dial 988, press 3

Trans Lifeline
Trans/nonbinary peer support, community, and resources.
Translifeline.org
(877) 565-8860

The Trevor Project
24/7 crisis intervention. Also has information, roundtables, and online spaces for queer teens to make friends.
thetrevorproject.org
trevorspace.org
Call: (866) 488-7386
Text "Start" to 678678
Chat: TrevorChat.org

FAITH

Welcoming Resources by National LGBTQ Task Force
Resources for news, training, and affirming faiths. Welcoming Resources site includes queer faith history and multi-faith database of affirming spiritual centers.
Thetaskforce.org (202) 393-5177
WelcomingResources.org

HOUSING & BASIC NEEDS

Covenant House
Provides welcoming, affirming, and safe housing, food, education, counseling, and more in many cities for youth facing homelessness.
CovenantHouse.org (800) 388-3888

HOUSING & BASIC NEEDS

School House Connection
Youth resources for housing, scholarships, school rights, transportation, meals, enrolling without a guardian, independent FASFA/Taxes, child care, etc.
Schoolhouseconnection.org
(202) 364-7392

US Department of Housing and Urban Development (HUD)
Lists food, housing, healthcare, and safety providers. Hotlines for HIV/AIDS, domestic violence, child abuse, substance abuse, and mental health.
Hudexchange.info/housing-and-homeless-assistance
(800) 569-4287

SCHOOL & EDUCATION

Gay, Lesbian, and Straight Education Network (GLSEN)
Helps create inclusive learning environments. Kits to empower school inclusion, resources for educators, and more.
GLSEN.org

GSA Network
Resources for GSAs, including online meetings, wellness activities, summer camps, leadership programs, etc. Networks nationwide GSAs.
GSANetwork.org

LGBTQ+ Student Scholarship Database
A list of college scholarships, fellowships and grants for queer students.
Hrc.org/resources/scholarships
(800) 777-4723

Network Campus Pride
Resources for safe, inclusive colleges and universities. Has a queer friendly campus database, scholarship database, FASFA dependency override guide, and support for fraternity/sorority life, athletics, careers, faith, health, minorities, etc.
Campusprideindex.org
(704) 277-6710

HEALTH & WELL-BEING

Born This Way Foundation
Resources for youth mental health, self-care, body image, bullying, addiction, etc.
Bornthisway.foundation

Fighting Eating Disorders in Underrepresented Populations (FEDUP)
Provides community healing, education, and support to gender-diverse and trans individuals with eating disorders.
Fedupcollective.org

HIV Positive Magazine
Resources for HIV-positive people, including guides, medical support, and places providing services.
HIVpositivemagazine.com

LGBTQ and All
Directory of queer-friendly therapists, gender confirmation surgeons, and treatment centers. Also has wellness and mental health blogs, guides, and community resources.
LGBTQandAll.com

US Substance Abuse and Mental Health Services Administration
Database of mental health and substance abuse treatment centers.
Findtreatment.gov (800) 662-4357

LEGAL

GLBTQ Legal Advocates & Defenders
Provides free, confidential legal information, referrals, and assistance, and issues/state resource search tool.
GLAD.org (800) 455-GLAD

National Center for Lesbian Rights
LGBTQ+ advocates. Has a helpline, forum, and legal referrals for low-income clients.
NCLrights.org (800) 528-6257

Transgender Law Center
Advocates for law and policy changes. Also provides help and referrals for legal challenges such as healthcare, immigration, IDs, etc.
TransgenderLawCenter.org
(510) 587-9696